Hiking
Michigan

by
Mike Modrzynski

FALCON™

Falcon Press® Publishing Co., Inc.
Helena, Montana

A **FALCON** GUIDE

Falcon Press is continually expanding its list of recreational guidebooks. All books include detailed descriptions, accurate maps, and all the information necessary for enjoyable trips. You can order extra copies of this book and get information and prices for other Falcon guidebooks by writing Falcon Press, P.O. Box 1718, Helena, MT 59624 or calling toll free 1-800-582-2665. Also, please ask for a free copy of our current catalog.

©1996 by Falcon Press Publishing Co., Inc.,
Helena and Billings, Montana.

Printed in the United States of America.

All black-and-white photos by author unless stated otherwise.
Cover photo by Larry Mishkar, F-Stock.

Library of Congress Cataloging-in-Publication Data

Modrzynski, Mike
    Hiking Michigan / by Mike Modrzynski.
       p.   cm.
    ISBN 1-56044-226-3 (pbk. : alk. paper)
    1. Hiking—Michigan—Guidebooks. 2. Michigan—Guidebooks.
I. Title.
GV199.42.M5M63   1996
796.5'1'09774—dc20   96-1004
                                          CIP

CAUTION

Outdoor recreation activities are by their very nature potentially hazardous. All participants in such activities must assume the responsibility for their own actions and safety. The information contained in this guidebook cannot replace sound judgment and good decision-making skills, which help reduce the risk exposure, nor does the scope of this book allow for disclosure of all the potential hazards and risks involved in such activities.

Learn as much as possible about the outdoor recreation activities you participate in, prepare for the unexpected, and be safe and cautious. The reward will be a safer and more enjoyable experience.

 Text pages printed on recycled paper.

CONTENTS

OVERVIEW MAP vi

LEGEND vii

INTRODUCTION 1

    Using This Guide 1

    Camping on State and Federal Lands 3

    Clothing and Equipment 5

    Water: Is It Safe? 6

    Wildlife 6

    Leave No Trace 9

MICHIGAN'S RAILS-TO-TRAILS PROGRAM 10

EXTENDED HIKES

    1 — *North Country Trail* 13

    Lower Peninsula 15

    Upper Peninsula 20

Isle Royale National Park 23

    2 — *Greenstone Ridge Trail* 26

    3 — *Minong Ridge Trail* 28

    4 — *Feldmann Ridge-island Mine Loop* 29

    5 — *Rock Harbor Trail* 31

    6 — *Indian Portage Trail* 31

    7 — *Huginnin Cove Loop* 32

    8 — *Ishpeming Trail* 34

    Additional Trails 35

Porcupine Mountains Wilderness State Park 37

    9 — *Lake Superior Trail* 40

    10 — *Little and Big Carp River Trails* 42

    11 — *Government Peak Trail* 43

    12 — *Lost Lake Trail* 44

    13 — *Correction Line Trail* 46

    14 — *Mirror Lakes Trails* 46

    15 — *Pinkerton Creek Trail* 47

    16 — *Cross Trail* 48

17 — *Escarpment Trail* 49

Additional Trails 50

18 — *Sylvania Wilderness & Recreation Area* 52

19 — *Bay de Noc-Grand Island Trail* 57

Lower Peninsula

20 — *High Country Pathway* 61

    Clear Lake Nature Trail 66

    Sinkhole Pathway 68

    Shingle Mill Pathway 70

    Jackson Lake Hiking Trail 72

21 — *Shore-to-Shore Trail* 73

22 — *Waterloo-Pinckney Recreation Hiking Trail* 79

    Waterlooo Recreation Area 82

WEEKEND HIKES

Upper Peninsula

23 — *Cedar River Pathway* 85

24 — *Seney National Wildlife Refuge* 88

25 — *Fox River Pathway* 92

Lower Peninsula

Sleeping Bear Dunes National Lakeshore *96*

26 — *Good Harbror Bay Loop* 97

27 — *Pyramid Point Loop* 99

28 — *Bay View Hiking Trails* 101

29 — *Alligator Hill Trails* 104

30 — *Dunes Hiking Trails* 107

31 — *Shauger Hill Hiking Trails* 110

32 — *Windy Moraine Loop* 112

33 — *Old Indian Trails* 114

34 — *Empire Bluff Trail* 116

35 — *Platte Plains Trails* 117

36 — *Ocqueoc Falls Bicentennial Pathway* 120

37 — *Hoist Lakes Foot Travel Area* 124

38 — *Rifle River Recreation Area* 127

39 — *Proud Lake Recreation Area* 130
40 — *Island Lake Recreation Area* 132

NATURE HIKES
Upper Peninsula
41 — *Lake Gogebic State Park* 135
42 — *Days River Pathway* 137
Lower Peninsula
43 — *Herman Vogler Conservation Area* 140
44 — *Grass River Natural Area* 145
45 — *Pintail Pond Nature Trail* 148
46 — *Old Nursery Trail* 150
47 — *Tobico Marsh Trail* 152
48 — *Sleeper State Park* 155
49 — *Price Nature Center* 158
50 — *For-Mar Nature Preserve* 160
51 — *Woldumar Nature Center* 162
52 — *Love Creek County Park & Nature Center* 165

APPENDIX A
A Hiker's Checklist 169

APPENDIX B
Sources For More Information 171

OVERVIEW MAP

LEGEND

Interstate	(00)
U.S. Highway	(00)
State or Other Principal Road	(000)
Forest Road	[0000]
Interstate Highway	⇒
Paved Road	⇒
Unpaved Road	⇒
Unimproved Road	= = = = = = ⇒
Trailhead/Parking	○ (P)
Lookout Tower	⊡

Main Trail(s)	------------------
Alternate/ Secondary Trails	------------------
River	～～～
Lake	
Marsh	↯ ↯
Campground	▲
Bridge	⏝
Cabins/Buildings	■

N

0   0.5   1
Miles

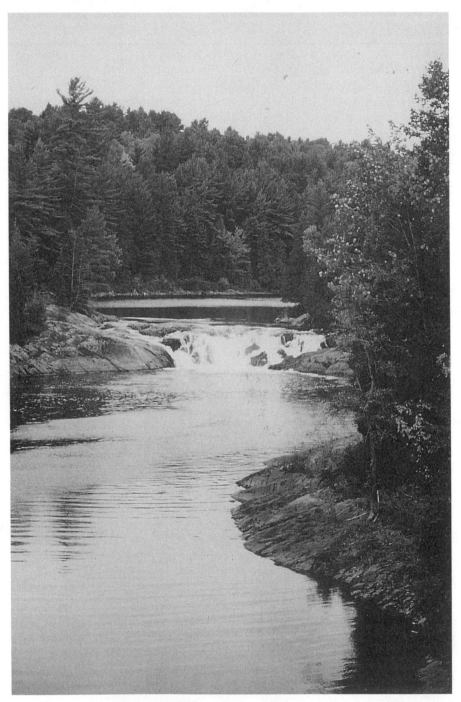

Small waterfalls are common sights along the northern shoulders of the Upper Peninsula.

INTRODUCTION

Michigan's many trails run the gamut from urban walks to total wilderness treks. Spreading across two peninsulas, they afford hikers the chance to explore the mixed history of the patchwork quilt called "The Wolverine State" in a day, weekend, or entire summer. Hundreds of trails lace the Michigan countryside, providing hiking opportunities along sandy or cliff shores of four of the five Great Lakes, or in the region's northern mountains, or in its vast forests.

Hikers who have a spirit of adventure and a taste for wilderness will find trails in the state's Upper Peninsula to their liking—especially those in the Porcupine Mountains, or on stark and beautiful Isle Royale, alone in Lake Superior. The Lower Peninsula provides its own brand of accessible wilderness, the crowning jewel of which is the High Country Pathway through Pigeon River State Forest in the northern half of lower Michigan's "mitten." And for those with a summer to while away, there is always the state's 875-mile stretch of the national North Country Trail, which guides hikers across Michigan's full spectrum.

Trail users in Michigan also benefit from a union with the state Department of Natural Resources (DNR), which has helped preserve and extend the web of trails in the state through its Rails-to-Trails Program. The rail trails and other Michigan routes meander through historic lumber camps long ago reclaimed by forest, go across giant tracts of wetlands and their fragile ecosystems, and head into the heart of wilderness. Stand on the ridges of Isle Royale and wonder at the insignificance of human life in the midst of Lake Superior's power and beauty. Marvel at the breathtaking view from the overlook above Lake of the Clouds in the Porcupine Mountains. These experiences and more are found along the thousands of trail miles that Michigan offers.

This book is by no means a complete inventory of Michigan's hiking trails, but it does look at each of the state's regions and opens doors in each area. One person could spend a lifetime hiking the hundreds of available trails and, given the DNR's commitment to open new routes, the task would be never-ending. Hikers who want to begin somewhere can take this guide in hand, take stock of their abilities and interests, then plan a hike in Michigan. The opportunities are endless.

Using This Guidebook

Some wilderness hikes in both the Upper and Lower peninsulas may require either time or a level of conditioning not in the grasp of the average hiker, but most trails can be handled by even the casual trekker. Most trails in Michigan require more determination than skill—more grit than guts—to complete. But don't ever underestimate the hazards of careless hiking. Plan ahead, and know your limitations.

The hikes described in this book are organized into three sections based on hikers' time limitations, not trail difficulty. The **extended hikes** described in the first section are just that—longer hikes that will require extended stays

A view of Lake of the Clouds. Michigan Department of Natural Resources (DNR), Parks and Recreation Division photo.

in the backcountry. These routes demand reliance on camping and other outdoor skills. **Weekend hikes** are, in many cases, just shorter versions of an extended hike, and often call on many of the same skills and knowledge. **Nature hikes** offer short routes for families and inexperienced hikers who nevertheless want to enjoy the outdoors.

The main intent of this guide is to provide information that helps hikers choose trails that match their desires and abilities. Each entry provides a detailed description of a trail and notes its natural and historic features. Each trail description begins with an outline of the physical characteristics of the trail, for quick and easy reference.

A general description comes first. This brief description is followed by notes on trail difficulty, which can be interpreted as follows: **Easy** trails are relatively short, flat, and well marked, and they can be completed without difficulty by hikers of all abilities; **moderate** trails will challenge novices with steeper grades or navigational requirements; **difficult** routes will tax experienced hikers in grades, route-finding, and/or length.

Entries also list suggested maps and give the address for the managing agency(s), compiled in Appendix B. Use this guide in partnership with local area maps, topographic quads, and other resources, such as those listed. Be prepared to use a compass and map on strenuous hikes, extended hikes, and many wilderness hikes.

After the initial reference notes, each hike entry features a mile-by-mile description of landmarks, trail junctions, and environments. This section tells hikers what to expect along the trail, and also offers tips on safety, common

Michigan's trail systems track across much of the state's rural back country.

weather occurrences, wildlife, and more. The maps and photographs in this book may also help you get a feel for the trails before you hike them.

Camping on State and Federal Lands

Camping along many of the trails in Michigan is restricted to designated campgrounds, but on many of the more remote systems, on both state and federal lands, hikers have some freedom in selecting a spot to pitch a tent. A few restrictions, however, may apply; these are designed to preserve the environment along the trails and to maintain the rustic nature of trails such as the North Country Trail and the High Country Pathway.

Several areas have specific regulations regarding camping. For instance, the Sylvania Wilderness, a hidden gem of the Upper Peninsula, allows camping only in developed locations around each of its lakes. Camping is allowed in designated sites under USDA Forest Service regulations that restrict the number of campers and regulate campfires, cooking, and firewood gathering.

In most state and federal forests, the rules are more lenient, permitting hikers to select their own campsites with only a few restrictions as to where they might be placed. Campsites must be at least 200 feet from lakes, streams, and/or wetlands, and construction of any sort of permanent structure is prohibited; that includes a toilet facility. Soapy water must be disposed of at least 200 feet from any water source, and bathing in streams or lakes is prohibited.

The Mackinac Bridge, Michigan's most famous landmark, connects its two peninsulas and its hundreds of miles of trails.

For detailed information, contact:
Michigan Department of Natural Resources
Forest Management Division
P.O. Box 30452
Lansing, Michigan 48909-7952

Michigan Department of Natural Resources
Parks and Recreation Division
P.O. Box 30028
Lansing, Michigan 48909

Hikers may also want to write or call the specific references for each area, as mentioned in the "For More Information" section of each hike entry or listed in Appendix B.

Clothing and Equipment

Hikers who are unused to Michigan's variable weather should plan for all types of climate. Dress warmly, in waterproof and wicking layers, especially in wilderness areas such as the Porcupine Mountains or Isle Royale. Lakeshore weather and wilderness experiences require that visitors plan for the probability of cool, damp evenings.

Hypothermia, the dangerous lowering of the body's core temperature, is not usually considered a danger during the milder hiking seasons in Michigan.

Camping along the Escarpment Trail. Michigan DNR, Parks and Recreation Division photo.

But it is a real problem year-round, and can happen without the usual accompaniment of bone-chilling temperatures. Hikers can become hypothermic in temperatures just below 50 degrees Fahrenheit, if conditions are right. Particularly in spring and fall, hypothermia can arrive dramatically; before you know it, you can be well on your way to trouble.

Avoid this real threat by recognizing that conditions that can create hypothermia exist throughout the year. Avoid chilling sweat by planning ahead, and pacing yourself to avoid overexertion. During a hike, stop as often as necessary to catch up with the effects weather or hard work is having on your body, and carry extra rain gear and clothing to replace damp or sweat-soaked garb.

Water: Is It Safe?

Water is one item hikers will find in great amounts in Michigan, but none of it should be considered safe enough to drink as found. As pure as the brooks and streams of wilderness areas may seem, do not attempt to drink from them without first boiling or filtering the water.

Streams, brooks, and springs are all home to a large number of bacteria, protozoa, and viruses. In Michigan, the most notable, and potentially hazardous, is the protozoan *Giardia lamblia*, an intestinal parasite that has spoiled more hikes than anything except, maybe, the weather. Giardia thrives in cold, clear streams and lakes, and is carried in the intestines and feces of beaver, muskrat, moose, and other animals that rely on water for existence.

Wildlife

One of the benefits of hiking in Michigan is the chance to observe its wildlife. The state is home to more than two hundred species of songbirds, plus one of the largest herds of white-tailed deer in the United States and the largest free-roaming herd of elk east of the Mississippi River. Hikers may see coyotes, foxes, raccoons, wild turkeys, rabbits, and other small game.

The state also is home to two major predators, the wolf and the black bear. Wolves are common only in Isle Royale National Park, although they have been sighted in portions of the western Upper Peninsula. Black bears are found in nearly every county in the state. Hikers must take precautions to avoid confrontations with either wolves or bears, especially when camping or transporting food.

Face-to-face encounters with either predator are unlikely, but both wolves and bears are attracted to food sources, including garbage. They may also be met on the trail; hikers should avoid travel routes favored by bears (look for scat as a warning) and should hike during the day, when bears are least active. A few more tips for hiking in bear country:

- Stay on established trails, and make noise while traveling.
- Avoid hiking during the early morning and late evening.
- Don't camp in an area obviously frequented by bears. If you see a bear or fresh sign where you intend to camp, pick another site.
- Set up your tent or sleeping area away from cooking areas.

Hanging food on a "bear pole" at Mirror Lake. Michigan DNR, Parks and Recreation Division photo.

The Pigeon River Country State Forest is home to the state's elk herd.

- Keep a clean camp, and avoid food odors. Lock food in a vehicle or suspend it from a nearby tree. Double-bag garbage to avoid attracting uninvited guests.
- Do not camp near game trails.
- If possible, camp near trees that can be climbed if a bear pursues you. You can't outrun a bear, so don't plan to. Although black bears do climb trees, some defense is better than no defense.

Our wild state also includes a variety of smaller, flying critters that inspire human discomfort. There never seems to be a time—except for frozen winter—when there isn't some kind of bug around to cause problems. In early spring, wet areas are the natural breeding grounds for many of the worst winged pests. Once the hordes of black flies disappear in mid-June, mosquitos thrive on the scene. And, of course, there is always the ever-present tick to keep things interesting.

A little bug dope will go a long way. Using repellents can be the most effective preventative measure, but be sure to use appropriate ones that meet your specific needs. Be aware of the effects and contents of the repellents you use, to avoid compounding medical problems or risking your health. Using DEET or permethrin on clothing and a lotion repellent on your skin builds a most effective anti-insect system.

Basic guidelines for avoiding most bugs:
- Spray clothing and other gear with permethrin before you leave for your hike.
- Use lotions, sprays, or creams on exposed skin.

The most common animal along the pathway, the white-tailed deer, shares this diverse habitat of the region with black bear, turkey, and elk.

- Use specific repellents for specific bugs. Not all repellents work on all species. Citronella works against mosquitos, for instance, but is useless against black flies.
- Keep in mind that strong chemical repellents may be irritants and, in some cases, endanger your health. Use them sparingly and wisely.

Besides wolves, bears, and insects, Michigan hikers have one other living trail hazard: the Massasauga rattlesnake, or swamp rattler, the state's only poisonous snake. Massasauga rattlers are small, mild-mannered snakes found in wet and low-lying areas. They are dark, spotted, and hard to spot in the undergrowth. Rarely seen outside a swamp environment, these small snakes are prevalent throughout the state but most common in the northeastern Lower Peninsula.

Leave No Trace

Conscientious hikers don't need the reminder, and others probably won't read it, but here it is nevertheless: Garbage does not change its character in a wilderness setting. The motto "Pack It In, Pack It Out" is the golden rule of responsible hiking. Remember that glass, aluminum foil, and disposable juice containers are not meant for burning in backcountry campfires, and that cigarette butts and candy wrappers seem never to disappear. Our obligation to respect and protect the trailside environment means that we all must do our part to ensure the terrain we travel retains no record of our passing. To keep wilderness beautiful and remote, and to maintain our trails as a natural experience, please be aware of your impact on the land. Walk lightly, and leave no trace.

Michigan offers a lifetime of hiking opportunities, with trails stretching from shore to shore and along the length and width of two peninsulas. To make sure this treasure remains for future generations, take only pictures and memories.

MICHIGAN'S RAILS-TO-TRAILS PROGRAM

Michigan's extensive railroad system once linked logging operations, mines, and far-flung agricultural regions with the state's sprawling industrialized areas. In this century, many of these train tracks lapsed into disrepair, pushed into obscurity by reduced markets and a modern highway system. Today, many of these weed-choked lines with rotting ties and rusting rails have found new life as part of Michigan's Rails-to-Trails Program.

The Michigan Trailways Act, passed by the Michigan Legislature in 1993, authorized and encouraged creation of a trailway system along the state's 5,000 miles of unused rail lines. Local governments, organizations, private citizens, and the Department of Natural Resources (DNR) have worked together to create this multi-agency, multi-use trail network. Since 1970, the DNR and other agencies have reclaimed nearly 400 miles of the nearly 10,000 miles of tracks that once spread like a spider's web across both peninsulas. The program originally was intended to create snowmobile trails, but has benefited hikers, mountain bikers, and horse users as well. In time, state officials hope to double the number of available miles.

The rail trails are ideal for many uses. Their gentle grade changes and extended flat runs appeal to planners trying to include less-active or physically impaired hikers, as well as snowmobilers and bikers. They link diverse environments, passing through urban, rural, and even semi-wilderness settings. Where the trails pass deserted lumbering and mining towns, they are living historical pathways as well, providing educational opportunities along with recreation. In more remote areas, they open access to some of the state's out-of-the-way rivers and lakes, and are a means of reaching a natural laboratory of plants and wildlife otherwise undisturbed by the mechanized world.

Because they link several regions of the state, the rails-to-trails systems can help hikers create more accessible routes. Backcountry users can follow the lines to transform a closed-loop hike into a week-long trek across Michigan. The DNR's hope is to eventually link most major trails so trail users can begin outings at any number of points in an easy, convenient way.

DNR personnel have already acquired a large number of rail corridors or segments as parts of the spreading snowmobile trail system that covers much of northern Michigan. This has been a three-season bounty for hikers and other non-mechanized users. The fifteen "snowmobile" routes amount to nearly 300 miles of public trails in dry seasons. These are mainly located in the Upper Peninsula, but include one 23-mile segment linking Mackinaw City to Alanson in the Lower Peninsula.

Other Rails-to-Trails sections include:

- **The Hart-Montague Trail**, which winds for 21 miles across portions of Oceana and Muskegon counties in western Michigan. The property was donated to the state by a private citizen and in 1988 was designated Hart-Montague State Park. The entire length of the trail has recently been paved to open it to more users.
- **The Kal-Haven Trail and Sesquicentennial State Park**, another reclaimed rail corridor linking metropolitan Kalamazoo and South Haven in southwestern Michigan. This 38-mile paved trail is open to all modes of non-mechanized travel spring through fall, and open to snowmobiles once there is sufficient snow cover. The public Friends of the Kal-Haven Trail group is a strong force behind the improvement and care of this right-of-way.
- **The Paint Creek Trail**, which offers access to one of southern Michigan's finest blue-ribbon trout fisheries and is free of the antagonizing din of motorized pests. The 8.5-mile trail isn't paved, but has been improved with a gravel cap that makes hiking easy, even for anglers in waders. The trail links Lake Orion and Rochester, providing a quiet getaway near an urban setting. A 0.5-mile stretch of right-of-way recently purchased by the DNR connects this placid trail to the Rochester-Utica Recreation Area.
- **Lakelands Trail State Park**, a 31-mile stretch of pathway linking the communities of Jackson and Hamburg in southern Michigan
- **The South Lyon to Wixom** right-of-way, a 7-mile corridor in western Oakland County that DNR officials hope to eventually link to the Lakelands system.
- **Bay City to Pinconning** right-of-ways, which contain two short segments of abandoned railbed. The first is a 3.7-mile segment located next to the Nayanquing Point Wildlife Area and is presently managed by the DNR Wildlife Division. The other, shorter segment is a 2-mile stretch connecting Bay City State Park with Tobico Marsh State Game Area.

In Oakland County, a 4-mile stretch of rail line in West Bloomfield Township will eventually be joined to other non-mechanized trails in the region. Midland County now owns a right-of-way that will eventually link Midland to Clare.

Since 1992, the DNR has added three other major abandoned rail segments to the Rails-to-Trails inventory and, according to Phillip Wells of the DNR Parks and Recreation Division, these will soon be joined by others. The longest segment, the Grand Rapids to Cadillac Line or "White Pine Trail," as it is known locally, goes for 90 miles through diverse ecosystems. The east-west Clare to Baldwin line adds another 50 miles to the inventory.

Brief but vital to the program in southwest Michigan are the 16 miles of rail grade from South Haven to Hartford. This short segment will become part of the Kal-Haven Trail. It runs through farmland and forest, and is quite remote. The Parks and Recreation Division will manage the trail as a unit of Van Buren State Park, 2 miles away, which may someday be linked to the path by a trail spur.

Approval has also been given to purchase two short segments of rail corridor in Pellston and Brutus in Emmet County, to bridge gaps in the 23-mile trail connecting Mackinaw City to Alanson. The DNR plans to develop the complete corridor as a multi-use trail system and, eventually, extend it into Petoskey.

Thus far, there are more than 225 miles of completed or designated railbed trails in Michigan's Lower Peninsula. The DNR has proposed adding another 500 miles of abandoned rail corridor to the inventory. The department already owns 300 miles of abandoned right-of-way in the Upper Peninsula, used primarily by snowmobilers. "Since the DNR started adding these segments to the trail systems, we have been full speed ahead," Phillip Wells said. "We intend to keep following the basic guidelines of the program as long as we continue to get such great local support."

Michigan rail line right-of-ways are being abandoned at a rate of more than 100 miles each year. These segments are being incorporated into state or local recreation areas as they become available, contributing to the state's Rails-to-Trails Program. For more information on the official Rails-to-Trails Program, contact:

Phillip Wells
Rails-to-Trails Program
Michigan Department of Natural Resources
Forest Management Division
P.O. Box 30028
Lansing, Michigan 48909
(517) 335-3040

Overview

Michigan's 875-mile segment of the national North Country Trail (NCT) crosses varied terrain and habitats. The entire trail route carves through seven states, linking Crown Point, New York, with Lake Sakakawea, North Dakota, over a distance of some 3,200 miles. Michigan contains the longest part of the route, which follows roads and certified trail sections from the Ohio-Michigan border near the town of Morenci to the Upper Peninsula community of Ironwood, at Wisconsin's edge.

The NCT passes through farmland, forests, urban areas, and even wilderness as it makes its way west. Nearly sixty percent of the trail in Michigan is certified, and work continues on the remaining miles, most of which are in southern Michigan where large tracts of private land complicate trail routing. Much of the lower trail system follows county roads, but hikers reaching Newaygo County will find major certified segments guiding them to the Straits of Mackinac and into the wilder Upper Peninsula. The east-west trail across the U.P. often follows the shore of Lake Superior.

The NCT is the most diverse of Michigan's trails, offering sections that can be easily handled by the casual hiker and, around the next turn, present challenges best handled by only veteran hikers. It offers a challenge of epic proportions for serious hikers who take on its entire length. But it also is a fine resource for casual hikers who want to take shorter, easier hikes and walk only segments of the system.

The route is a great way to see much of what Michigan has to offer. One of its special attractions is the Mackinac Bridge, a 5-mile suspension bridge connecting the two peninsulas. A shuttle bus carries hikers across the bridge, which can be dangerous in windy conditions. Other highlights include Mackinac Island, a history-rich island reached by a short boat ride where only horse, bike, and foot travel is allowed; Tahquamenon Falls, the second-largest waterfall east of the Mississippi River; Pictured Rocks National Lakeshore; and Porcupine Mountains State Park, which can be reached via a short detour from Trap Falls near Norwitch, west of Munising.

General description: An 875-mile linear route across the state, part of a national scenic trail from New York to North Dakota.
General location: Intermittent trails and roads from the southern Lower Peninsula through the western Upper Peninsula.
Maps: Lower Peninsula—Croton Dam to Hodenpyle Dam (the Manistee National Forest); Interlochen to Boyne Falls. Upper Peninsula—Saint Ignace to Harvey (Hiawatha National Forest); and Marquette to Ironwood (Ottawa National Forest) available through the North Country Store, P.O. Box 311, White Cloud, MI 49349. County road maps are available through the Department of

1   NORTH COUNTRY TRAIL

Natural Resources (DNR), Information Services Center, Box 30028, Lansing, MI 48909, and from individual counties (see Appendix B).

Degree of difficulty: Most Lower Peninsula sections of the NCT are easy to moderate. Upper Peninsula trails include several moderate sections, but the trail's extreme western third is difficult. The condition of the trail varies greatly, and hikers should be aware of the difficulty of hiking in soft sand along the shores of Lakes Michigan and Superior.

Length: 875 miles in its entirety, but this can be broken into shorter hikes to fit any timetable. The NCT is a linear trail, so make arrangements to return to a start point or retrace your steps.

Elevations: Lower Peninsula trails are generally flat, with rolling terrain midway up the peninsula's west side. The U.P.'s eastern half mixes rolling hills and flat stretches; its western half presents rocky climbs and varied elevations that can turn leisure into grueling effort.

Special attractions: A complete look at urban and rural Michigan, including Mackinac Bridge, Mackinac Island, Tahquamenon Falls, Pictured Rocks National Lakeshore, Porcupine Mountains.

Best season: Year-round, but snowy weather in the northern portion precludes hiking in winter months. Late summer and early fall are perhaps the best times. Hunters may be in the area from September 15 until well after the first snowfall.

For more information: Virginia Wunsch, North Country Trail Association, P.O. Box 311, White Cloud, MI 49349.

Finding the trailheads: Literally hundreds of trailheads exist for the NCT in Michigan, given the number of road crossings and cross-trails. The two main trailheads are at Morenci in the Lower Peninsula and Ironwood in the Upper Peninsula.

To find the unofficial Morenci trailhead, take Ranger Road 0.5 mile west of the Morenci airport until you reach the Michigan-Ohio border. The trail follows an abandoned railroad right-of-way.

To reach the Ironwood trailhead, take U.S. Highway 2 into Ironwood from Wisconsin. The on-road trailhead is at the highway bridge over the Montreal River. Hikers looking for a nearby off-road trailhead will need to use Gogebic County road maps to get from Ironwood west to County Road 219. The trailhead is on the banks of the Black River.

The hikes: The trail enters Michigan near Morenci in the southeastern corner of the state. From there it heads northwest through both urban and rural settings toward certified trail segments in Manistee National Forest. It then takes a decided turn northward through the Jordan Valley and Wilderness State Park to cross the Straits of Mackinac.

The Upper Peninsula segment of the trail system goes east to west starting in Hiawatha National Forest. It passes Tahquamenon Falls State Park, Pictured Rocks National Lakeshore, and parts of Ottawa National Forest before it exits Michigan at the town of Ironwood.

The hike description below goes south to north, and gives only a general overview of the path's various sections. Hikers who intend to walk the entire route should contact the sources listed above for more detailed information, especially county road maps and information on cabin rental or camping facilities.

Lower Peninsula

The North Country Trail (NCT) enters Michigan from Ohio at a point west of the city of Morenci. Since the southern third of the route is not yet certified, the official trailhead has yet to be pinpointed. The generally accepted starting point is about 4 miles southwest of Morenci at an abandoned railroad grade that crosses the state border. Hikers should arm themselves with county road maps for Lenawee and Hillsdale counties to help navigate the small, established trails along this initial, rural section.

From Morenci, hikers should follow county roads north to the only planned segment of the NCT in the area, at Lake Hudson State Recreation Area, which is not yet complete. For those who want to make a base camp somewhere near the trail's south end, camping is available in the Lake Hudson recreation area.

From Lake Hudson, NCT hikers go west to enter the Lost Nations State Game Area—which offers only a point of reference, not a reliable trail system. Hikers should follow their own maps and compasses to go still farther west to the next established trail, the 5-mile Baw Beese Trail near the city of Osseo. The Baw Beese section of trail follows an abandoned railroad grade to Waterworks Park in Hillsdale. This short link in the NCT is an example of the state's Rails-to-Trails Program. Contact the Hillsdale City Recreation Department for information on the availability of camping or lodging in the area.

Beginning at the Hillsdale city limits, hikers travel the first certified segments of the NCT, the 3-mile Michigan Highway 99 Bikeway, connecting Hillsdale with Jonesville. This short, paved bikeway, open to hikers, parallels M-99. From its end in Jonesville, hikers must again set their own routes along county roads, heading generally northwest for more than 40 miles through Hillsdale and Calhoun counties. They should aim for the Battle Creek Linear Parkway, an 8-mile hike through downtown Battle Creek that leads to an interesting stop at Fort Custer National Cemetery. The cemetery, some 5 miles west of Battle Creek, is just 0.25 mile from the community of Augusta, a great place to stop for a night. Hikers looking for a rest will find cabins for rent on the nearby lake.

From Augusta the trail continues northwest. Once again you'll need county road maps to pick a route. Make your way through Kalamazoo and Barry counties to reach the next navigation point, the Barry State Game Area. From the game area, head on to Yankee Springs State Park, 9 miles west of Hastings on County Road A42. The area contains a number of small trail loops and is open year-round with cabins for rent within the park. Note that camping space is at a premium for much of the southern NCT; hikers should call ahead to make arrangements.

Once out of Yankee Springs, hikers will have to deal with county roads again, this time heading north through urban Kent County. You will encounter short links in the NCT at Siedman Park and Egypt Valley, accounting for 7.5 miles of prepared trails. The terrain here is rolling, and the hikes are rated moderate, so take your time. Water is available at Siedman Park only.

The next 20 miles are road miles. Hikers reach the next NCT section at Rogue River State Game Area in northern Kent County. They then go back to county roads to cross into Newaygo County until they reach Croton Dam near the city of Newaygo, some 12 miles from the county line. Camping is available at Croton Dam Pond Campground, 1 mile north.

The stretch of trail leading from Croton Dam is a chain of county roads in Newaygo County that eventually lead past the west side of Twinwood Lake before it bends north and crosses Michigan Highway 37. Total distance of this segment is 7 miles.

The next 40 miles of trail have been NCT-certified. The path heads north-northwest for about 15 miles, crossing the White River Bridge just past Echo Road; a campground can be found 1 mile east. The trail crosses Michigan Highway 20, then Three Mile Road. From there, it's a 3.5-mile meander northwest to Five Mile Road. In this section, camping is permitted 200 feet off the trail, but be certain you are not on private land before setting up camp. There is a special stopover point for NCT hikers 7 miles northwest of White Cloud, about 1.5 miles from the trail: the North Country Trail Association headquarters-hostel, at the corner of Felch Road and Five Mile Rd., offering both hot showers and the latest trail information. The building is not always manned, but hikers can call (616) 689-1912 to arrange for use of the building.

Hikers can pick up the trail from the NCTA hostel and again head north-northwest. The trail continues in the same direction for more than 15 miles, passing around the west side of Nichols Lake and eventually crossing Thirteen Mile Road, also known as Cleveland Drive. The NCT takes a northeast heading from Thirteen Mile Rd. and passes several small lakes on a 2-mile leg to Highbank Lake (where there is a small campground). Hikers should follow Forest Road 5541 and Star Lake Road to reach the next checkpoint at Carrs Road in Lake County; there is a small campground on the Pere Marquette River about 1.5 miles east.

From the checkpoint, head northwest for 4 miles through Manistee National Forest to South Branch Road. The trail then winds north, then northwest, for 14 miles to Lake Road. Much of this leg of the trail goes through national forest, and camping is permitted 200 feet away from the trail on state or federal land. Hikers will have to follow Lake Road for 6 miles west until they reach Elk Highway, then take Campbell Road some 10.5 miles north and west. Use the Campbell Rd. bridge to get across the Little Manistee River and continue for about 2 miles to Forest Road 5337.

About 5 miles from the FR 5337 junction in Manistee County, the trail crosses Michigan Highway 55 and turns northeast for a 1.5-mile trek to Pine Creek Road, then an additional 2-mile jaunt to Chicago Road. The stretch from M-55 to Chicago Road partly crosses private land. It's only 2 miles more to the High Bridge Road and the Manistee River crossing. The trail then turns east as the terrain turns hilly for the next 4.5 miles. From there, at Forest Road 5233, the trail turns north for 6 miles until it reaches Coates Road. Forest roads make up the next 15 miles until the trail crosses Michigan Highway 115 at a roadside park just inside Wexford County. From there the trail uses county roads for the 9-mile trek to Michigan Highway 37.

Across M-37, the NCT parallels the north bank of the Manistee River until it reaches Baxter Bridge, a distance of 15 miles. The terrain changes back to rolling pine plantations. Hills and several ravines can cause problems for hikers if energy levels are low. Stop if you need to. There is a state forest campground just south of Baxter Bridge; watch for the signs as you cross the bridge.

From the river, the trail takes a short 1-mile detour, traveling between

Wexford and Grand Traverse counties before rejoining the Manistee River trace then going a total distance of about 8 miles to join the Shore-to-Shore Trail (see Hike 20), which it follows for about 55 miles.

The Shore-to-Shore stretch can be hard on hikers because of the impact horses have had on the fragile, sandy trail. The route is marked with blue markers showing a footprint and a horseshoe. It is easy to follow, and signage is both accurate and visible. The trail heads north from Michigan Highway 186 toward the Boardman River, 6 miles away. From the river crossing, the trail heads east from Kalkaska County to Guernsey Lake, crossing U.S. Highway 131, about 2 miles north of the town of Kalkaska. Nearly all of the trail is in Pere Marquette State Forest. The Old US 131 State Forest Campground is on the north bank of the Manistee River at the Old US 131 crossing.

The final leg of the Shore-to-Shore section of trail ends at Magni Road in Kalkaska County, just after hikers ford the Boardman River. The river is seldom more than knee-deep except during the very early stages of spring run-off. Scheck's Place State Forest Campground is located at the river crossing. From the river crossing the NCT continues east for about 3 miles, passing along the southern shore of Manistee Lake to County Road 612.

Hikers travel on CR 612 for about 2 miles to Sunrise Trail Road, then 2 more miles to a fork in the pathway. Take the east branch, a continuation of the NCT that swings north for 7 miles, bypassing Pickerel, Indian, and Eagle lakes then on to Sand Lake. Pickerel Lake State Forest Campground is on the southeast side of the lake; just before reaching Sand Lake, hikers will enter Antrim County and Pigeon River State Forest. The property around Sand Lake is all private, so hikers must follow county roads to reach County Road 39, about 2 miles farther north. The trail heads north from CR 39 for about 1 mile before heading northwest for 5 miles to the west side of Five Lake. A 0.5-mile trail leads to a small campground at the north end of the lake.

About 5 miles west and north of the lake on county roads, the NCT joins the Jordan Valley Pathway at Landslide Overlook. The pathway leads to Cascade Creek and its crossing, 2 miles west. Hikers cross the Jordan River 2 miles farther northwest at Pinney Bridge; there is a DNR campground about 100 yards north of the bridge. Follow the north bank of the river for about 4 miles to the next checkpoint at River Road, then cross the river once more and head east, uphill, for the 2-mile hike to Deadman's Hill. The NCT turns north from Deadman's Hill and joins the Warner Creek Pathway 2.75 miles later.

The next major road crossing is Michigan Highway 32, about 1.5 miles north. North and east another 4 miles, the trail crosses U.S. Highway 131. County roads provide the path for the trail as it crosses into Charlevoix County on Kuzmick Road. Hikers will have to follow still more county roads to reach the next certified segment of the trail, which goes from the Charlevoix County line northeast in Emmet County, comprising nearly 35 miles of the NCT.

The next certified segment picks up at Wilderness State Park, west of Mackinaw City. Taking off from the west shore of Wycamp Lake, the NCT goes north for about 1 mile to a state forest campground, then continues another mile to the Lake Michigan shore at Sturgeon Bay. Follow Lakeshore Road for

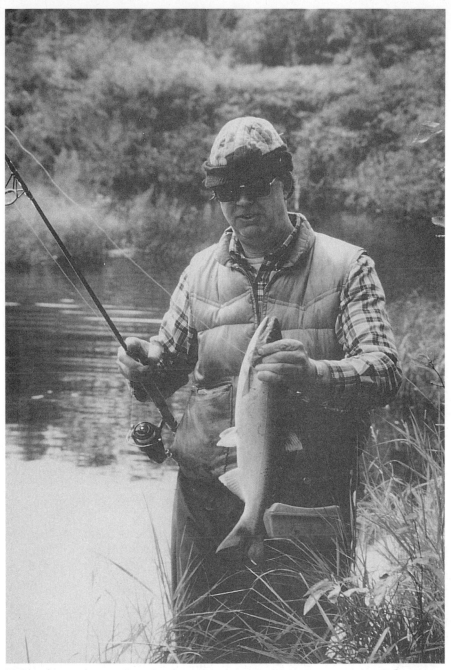

Fishing is a welcome diversion from the eight hundred miles of the North Country Trail.

3 miles to the junction with Lakeview Road. From this point travel north for about 2 miles to the boundary of the state park. The eastern boundary of Wilderness State Park is just over 5 miles away, but hikers may welcome a break from the rigors of the trail and want to spend a little time at this scenic northern park. You will have little trouble finding places to camp from here to the Straits of Mackinac. Wycamp Lake State Forest Campground is on the west side of the lake on the NCT, and Wilderness State Park offers 210 sites on Cecil Bay, about 0.5 mile off the trail. Leaving the park, hikers should follow the Spruce Ridge Trail east for about 2 miles to Cecil Bay Road. From there the trail winds through dense forests until it links up with an abandoned railroad grade that leads to Mackinaw City.

Unless you reach the Straits on Labor Day (the only time foot traffic is permitted on the Mackinac Bridge), you will have to find alternative methods to reach the Upper Peninsula. One way is to contact the Bridge Authority at (906) 643-7600 to arrange for a ride aboard the state-operated shuttle bus. Another is to ride a ferry boat across to Mackinac Island, then take another ferry over to Saint Ignace.

Upper Peninsula

Across the Straits, the trail picks up 1 mile from the bridge at an abandoned railroad grade in downtown Saint Ignace. The trail follows the grade for nearly 5 miles northwest out of the city before entering Hiawatha National Forest. About 6 miles farther, the track swings east of Brevoort Lake, then turns northeast for 2 miles until it crosses Worth Road. There are two primitive campgrounds nearby: 0.5 mile east, and 1 mile south. As on the rest of the NCT in Michigan, camping is permitted at least 200 feet off the trail on state or federal lands.

From here the trail takes a northern tack to the Carp River crossing, 8.5 miles away. About 8 miles north of the river, hikers will pass East Lake and Guard Lake. The trail turns north for about 6 miles to Trout Brook Pond. The NCT continues north along Biscuit Creek for nearly 5 miles before crossing the Pine River. The trail shadows the river for about 4 more miles west before swinging back to a northerly trace. There are two primitive campgrounds along the trail near the Pine River crossing. In 3 more miles, hikers pass Betchler Lakes. About 6 miles farther, the trail crosses Michigan Highway 28, and takes a northwesterly heading for 10.5 miles to the shores of Tahquamenon Bay on Lake Superior.

Hikers have to follow a sandy lakeshore for about 4 miles, then take forest roads for about 8 miles to the Tahquamenon River. Use the bridge on Michigan Highway 123 to cross the river, and continue west on the NCT. The lower set of Tahquamenon Falls are 12 miles from the M-123 bridge on the main trail. Hikers who have the time may want to plan an 8-mile side trip to the upper falls. Two state parks in the area offer camping: Tahquamenon Rivermouth State Park has 136 sites, and Tahquamenon Falls State Park has 183 sites.

From the falls, the NCT takes a decided westward trace for about 15 miles,

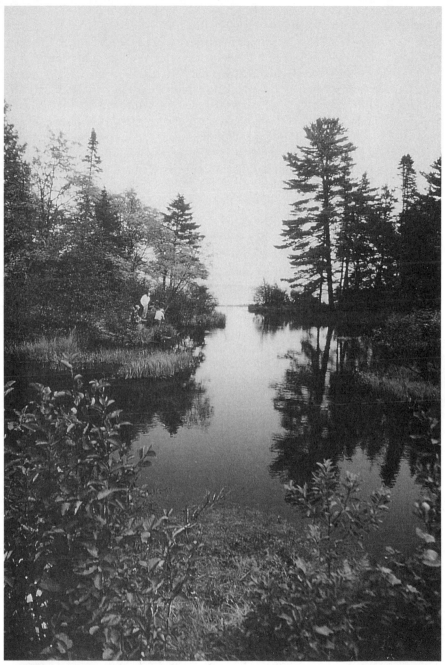

Upper Peninsula sections of the North Country Trail are scenic and laced with small streams.

crossing County Road 500 before turning north for 4 miles to Betsy River Road. About 4 miles north of that point, the NCT reaches the shore of Lake Superior near the mouth of the fabled Two Hearted River. It's a 3-mile hike to the river crossing, 5 miles to the Red and Green Bridge and a rustic campground.

Once across the Two Hearted River, the NCT parallels the Lake Superior shoreline for nearly 25 miles before turning south on County Road H58 for the 3-mile hike into the town of Grand Marais. It is 3 short miles from Grand Marais to Pictured Rocks National Lakeshore. From the park's visitor service center, the NCT traces 43 miles of shoreline trail, the high point of any visit to the Pictured Rocks region, including cliffs, sand dunes, and wilderness. The end of this segment of the trail is at Munising Falls. Camping and campgrounds are numerous along this stretch.

County Road H58 spills out into the city of Munising, about 2 miles from the falls. Follow Michigan Highways 28/94 south out of the city for about 1 mile to the M-28/M-94 fork, then turn south on M-94 to meet up with the NCT again. The next 24 trail miles follow a network of forest roads, crossing the Au Train River at the bridge on Forest Road 2276 and then the Laughing Whitefish River on the same road. From the Laughing Whitefish River, follow forest roads for about 4 miles until intersecting M-28. Follow M-28 west to its junction with U.S. Highway 41, then follow the paved bike path northwest into the city of Marquette.

Since the NCT is still under development in this area, hikers should follow M-28 west to the start of the next segment starting at Silver Lake Basin. This 18-mile stretch of the NCT ends in the parking lot of Craig Lake State Park. Camping is permitted in the park as long as you set up more than 150 feet from any lakeshore. Continue along M-28 west from this point until you reach the next checkpoint at Vermilac Road. On Vermilac Rd., go about 5 miles to the trailhead at the Plain Road bridge over the Sturgeon River. The NCT continues west along the north bank of the river, and the next 25 miles of the trail follow the rim of the Sturgeon River valley, then track through a portion of Ottawa National Forest. Hikers will have to wade the East Branch of the Ontonagon River near Gardner Road. Or, if the river is too high (or you just want to keep your feet dry), you can take a 3-mile detour along forest roads. One warning for campers: This is definitely black bear country. Hikers and campers must be aware that these animals are plentiful, and take necessary precautions.

From Gardner Road, the trail heads west once again toward U.S. Highway 45, 7 miles away, to a point near Victoria Dam. About 12 miles farther west, the NCT crosses the Gogebic Ridge Trail. Northwest, in 4 miles, the trail crosses Michigan Highway 64. The trail then turns north for about 3 miles, crosses the Big Iron River, and follows the north bank of the West Branch of the Big Iron for 8 miles until it reaches the boundary road of Porcupine Mountains State Park. The trail follows this road for 1 mile until it meets Summit Peak Road. Two smaller trails, Lily Pond and South Carp River, lead to the shores of Lake Superior.

Following the lakeshore, hikers will reach County Road 519. After 4 miles, the trail crosses Forest Road 117. From there, the trail winds for 5 miles to the Black River Campground, then hugs the west bank of the Black River for 5 miles to a point near Copper Peak Hill. Go 6 miles south on County Road 513, then 8 more miles past Auvignon Corner, to reach the city of Ironwood.

To reach Wisconsin, and its portion of the NCT, follow U.S. Highway 2 across the Montreal River. The trail starts at the bridge.

2-8 ISLE ROYALE NATIONAL PARK

Overview

Isle Royale is the largest freshwater island in the United States. In north-central Lake Superior, some 70 miles north of Houghton, Michigan, 49 miles north of Copper Harbor, Michigan, and 22 miles east of Grand Portage, Minnesota, it is still remote and wild. Access to the park is limited to air or water, so the stormy waters of Lake Superior can delay arrivals and departures. Allow a little latitude in your timetable when planning a trip to this isolated wilderness.

Isle Royale National Park was authorized by the U.S. Congress in 1931, "to conserve a prime example of Northwoods Wilderness." The park was designated part of the National Wilderness Preservation System in 1976, under the

The fragile environment of this rock-hard island creates panoramas unequalled anywhere in northern Michigan.

Wilderness Act, and remains today an example of primitive America. In 1981, Isle Royale was designated a Biosphere Reserve by the United Nations, recognizing the park's international significance. The park is made up of one large island and more than four hundred smaller islands. The main island, the namesake of the park, is 45 miles long and nearly 9 miles wide at its widest point.

As much as ninety-nine percent of the park has been designated as wilderness under the aegis of the National Park Service. The rugged nature of the terrain makes this one of the most picturesque settings a hiker could hope for. The park's outstanding isolation is protected by the island's location, and makes it an ideal natural laboratory; wolves and moose have been continuously studied on Isle Royale for the past three decades in the longest ongoing wildlife study anywhere in the world. The island supports populations of raptors, such as eagles, peregrine falcons, and ospreys, and large numbers of waterfowl. Fishermen find plenty of action in inland lakes and along offshore reefs; photographers are sometimes overwhelmed by the opportunities here. Add to these natural wonders the relics of man's early attempts to commercialize the island's resources—ancient copper mines and more—and you have a spectacular trip in store.

Approximately 165 miles of trails crisscross the 200-square-mile island. Hikes range from comfortable day hikes to cross-island excursions not recommended for anyone lacking experience, stamina, and, most importantly, the proper equipment. Since just getting to the island requires a level of commitment, the hikes in the park are rated as comfortably moderate to difficult, with a majority of the hikes falling midway between the two. The island's trail systems are well defined and easy to follow, with the exception of the Minong Ridge Trail, which offers a challenge to even seasoned hikers. Hikers on Isle Royale are limited primarily by time and determination—how willing they are to experience the wilderness.

The Isle Royale Topographic Map, sold in the region, is a more than adequate guide for hikers, but there are a number of specialized booklets available locally, including "Isle Royale National Park," by Jim DuFresne, which may assist first-time visitors. The staff at each of the visitor centers on the island can answer most questions.

Trail time estimates for Isle Royale have to be tempered with the unpredictable weather of the region. Most hikers will be able to maintain a 2-mile-per-hour pace, despite influences of constantly changing weather patterns caused by Lake Superior. In early summer, bugs can be a real problem in remote corners of the island. The later months of summer are the best months for hikers on the island, but it frequently rains during these warmer months, so be prepared. Daytime temperatures are often pleasant, and sometimes very warm, but nights can be cool, even chilly. During fall, evening temperatures can dip to nearly freezing. The park is open to visitors from mid-April until late October, so if visiting Isle Royale doesn't fit your summer vacation schedule, there is still plenty of time to hike the island's backcountry.

Elevations on the island are not a major factor on most hikes, although a tired hiker facing a steep 15- to 20-foot climb might argue the point. Major elevations are encountered along the Greenstone Ridge Trail, though. The six

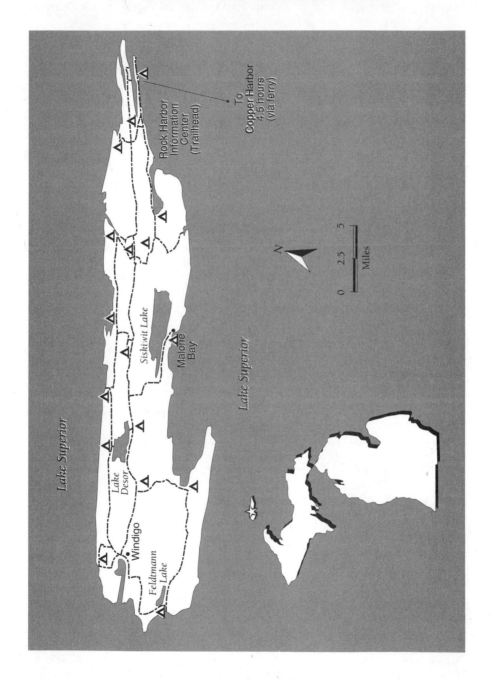

highest points are Sugar Mountain (1,362 feet), Mount Desor (1,394 feet), Ishpeming Point (1,377 feet), Mount Siskiwit (1,205 feet), Mount Ojibway (1,136 feet), and Mount Franklin (1,074 feet).

Off-trail travel is difficult on Isle Royale, since vegetation is thick and marshy areas make shortcuts nearly impossible to navigate. The fragile environment of the island has led to implementation of a low-impact camping policy in the park's thirty-six campgrounds. The guidelines for the policy are simply this: leave only footprints. Do not exaggerate your presence while hiking the park's trails. Remember, you are a visitor—an intruder—to the ecosystem.

Trailheads for the hikes around the island are, for all intents and purposes, the ferry docks that carry passengers from either Michigan or Minnesota to the island. The ferries make regular stops in various locations, providing access to the entire island so that hikers do not have to make lengthy cross-country treks. From Houghton, the *Ranger III* makes regular stops at the eastern landfall of Rock Harbor. At this landing, hikers will find an information center, meals, lodging, groceries, and other services like boat rentals. The *Isle Royale Queen III* sails from Copper Harbor, stopping also at Rock Harbor. The *Voyageur II*, sailing from Grand Portage, Minnesota, makes regular stops at Windigo, McCargoe Cove, Belle Isle, Rock Harbor, Daisy Farm, Chippewa Harbor, and Malone Bay. A second vessel, the *Wenonah*, also sails from Grand Portage, but has scheduled stops only at Windigo.

Other options are available through watercraft charters if you want to customize your visit to the park. For more information, contact National Park Concessions, Inc., (906) 337-4993.

2   GREENSTONE RIDGE TRAIL

General description: The park's most extensive trail, following the backbone of the main island.
General location: Isle Royale National Park.
Maps: Isle Royale Topographic Map.
Degree of difficulty: Difficult.
Length: 40 miles.
Elevations: Sugar Mountain, 1,362 feet; Mount Desor, 1,394 feet; Ishpeming Point, 1,377 feet; Mount Siskiwit, 1,205 feet; Mount Ojibway, 1,136 feet; Mount Franklin, 1,074 feet.
Special attractions: Dense forest and rugged wilderness, occasional views of Lake Superior, Lake Desor, Hatchet Lake.
Best season: Summer.
For more information: Park Superintendent, Isle Royale National Park, 87 North Ripley Street, Houghton, MI 49931; Isle Royale *Queen* Ferry, Copper Harbor, MI 49918, (906) 482-4950.
Finding the trailhead: Take the ferry to Windigo, on Isle Royale's west side, which is the trail's western trailhead and the last place hikers can pick up all

those necessary items they left behind on the mainland. The trail's eastern trailhead is at Lookout Louise.

The hike: The "Greenstone," as it's called here, is rated by many as the best of the Isle Royale hikes. The trail goes from Windigo, in the west, to Lookout Louise, in the east, traversing 40 miles of rugged beauty along the highest ridges of Isle Royale.

From the trailhead at Windigo, the trail rises to the first campground at Island Mine Campground, 6.3 miles to the east. The initial section of the trail is also the toughest of the entire trip; over the next 5.5 miles, hikers climb to the crest of Sugar Mountain (1,362 feet). The Island Mine Campground is a welcome sight after this ambitious start. To reach the campground you will have to make a 0.4-mile detour south onto the Island Mine Trail. The junction and the trail are well marked and easy to follow. Rest here; there's more work ahead.

Back on the main trail, hikers face a second steep ascent as they head for Mount Desor (1,394 feet), the highest elevation on the island, 1.5 miles east. Just over 3.5 miles east of this peak is the junction with a 0.25-mile spur trail running north to the Lake Desor Campground.

The next leg of the trail, from Lake Desor to Hatchet Lake, is 8 miles long, and not flat either. Hikers must scale yet another peak, Ishpeming Point (1,377 feet). The crest marks the halfway point of this leg—with the first half being the easier of the two. An observation tower marks the summit, but don't hope for much of a view around the island's thick foliage. Hikers have compared the final 4 miles of the Desor-Hatchet leg to a long roller coaster ride that makes the next campground a welcome sight. For the most part, thick forest blocks many of the views, even though you are hiking along the backbone of the park. Weary hikers finally reach the spur trail to the next campground on the shores of Hatchet Lake; the spur heads north off the main trail and goes for 0.5 mile.

The next leg of the trail includes still another peak, Mount Siskiwit (1,205 feet), but hikers won't have to climb it. That's little compensation, though—it's tough terrain along this trek to West Chickenbone Campground, nearly 8 miles east. The trail is not easy and will probably be the longest 8 miles you have hiked in some time. A satisfying element of this leg is that the views are quite good. The descent into the campground is fairly steep, dropping into a heavily forested area before reaching the junction with the campground spur trail.

Less than 2 miles farther east is the East Chickenbone Campground, so if the previous day's jaunt caused you to oversleep a bit, the next campground is just ahead . . . after all, some progress is better than no progress at all. The campground at East Chickenbone also marks the junction with the Minong Ridge Trail and the route to McCargoe Cove to the north.

From here on, the trail is fairly easy, although low-lying areas along the way have been known to spawn plenty of bugs in spring and early summer. It is about 4.5 miles to the a spur trail to the south, which leads to the Daisy Farm Campground. The 1.9-mile hike in is fairly easy; after a good night's sleep, hikers take a 1.7-mile hike along another spur trail that leads back to the main Greenstone route. The second spur trail rejoins the main trail at Mount Ojibway (1,136 feet). It is a fairly flat 2-mile hike to the final high point, Mount Franklin (1,074 feet). From here, it is an easy 4.8 miles to the eastern trailhead at Lookout Louise.

Hikers who have completed the Greenstone cross-island trek have two options: one, to arrange ahead of time for a boat to transport them across Tobin Harbor; or two, to backtrack to the junction with the Tobin Harbor Trail for a hike into Rock Harbor.

3   MINONG RIDGE TRAIL

General description: A cross-island hike along Minong Ridge to the Minong Mine and McCargoe Cove.
General location: Isle Royale National Park.
Maps: Isle Royale Topographic Map.
Degree of difficulty: Difficult.
Length: 29 miles.
Elevations: No significant elevations, but several ridges and strenuous sections.
Special attractions: McCargoe Cove, Todd Harbor, Little Todd Harbor, Lake Desor.
Best season: Summer.
For more information: Park Superintendent, Isle Royale National Park, 87 North Ripley Street, Houghton, MI 49931; Isle Royale Queen Ferry, Copper Harbor, MI 49918, (906) 482-4950.
Finding the trailhead: The trail begins at the ferry dock in McCargoe Cove; it ends at the Windigo ferry.

The hike: Starting at the eastern trailhead at McCargoe Cove is the gentle way to start this relatively difficult cross-island trek. From here, the first campground at Todd Harbor is a mere 6.6 miles west.

The first 4 miles of this leg more or less follow the rocky ridgelines and hiking can be difficult and the trail sometimes tough to keep track of. About 2 miles from the campground the trail leaves the ridgelines and drops into a thick forested area. The roller coaster doesn't stop, but the trail is more shaded.

The second segment is a bit less strenuous than the first. Its initial 1.5 miles are actually quite pleasant until you pass the junction with the Hatchet Lake Trail. Here, you become a ridge walker again and, although the trail is not nearly as imposing as the first leg, you will feel the same soreness by the end of the day. The final section of this part of the trail is a 0.5-mile descent to the campground at Little Todd Harbor. Look out for boggy areas, especially after a good rainfall.

Like a welcome respite, the third leg of the Minong Ridge Trail is a brief 6-mile trek to the next stop at the Lake Desor Campground. Hikers will spend nearly equal amounts of time along ridgelines and in forested areas as they continue westward. The trail does contain its share of ups and downs, but after nearly 6 miles the final descent starts at the junction with the spur trail leading to the campground 0.5 mile south of the main pathway.

The final 13 miles of trail are not terribly difficult, although they do require some special navigating through the wet areas. Ridge-hopping is somewhat less strenuous here. But it's the length of this part of the hike that takes the greatest toll on stamina. Hikers will pass several junctions with the east and west ends of the Huginnin Cove Loop and, later, will merge with the Greenstone before ending at Windigo.

Hikers anxious to get deep into the backcountry can start the hike at its western trailhead (Windigo), but prepare for a 12-mile hike to the first campground at Lake Desor, or opt for the hike north on the Huginnin Cove Trail and the campground there, about 5 miles from the trailhead. Keep in mind that if you choose to layover at Huginnin that first night, you will have another 5-mile hike facing you in the morning before you rejoin the Minong Ridge Trail.

4   FELDMANN RIDGE-ISLAND MINE LOOP

General description: A scenic three- or four-day loop departing from Windigo.
General location: Isle Royale National Park.
Maps: Isle Royale Topographic Map.
Degree of difficulty: Moderate to difficult.
Length: 24 miles.
Elevations: Red Oak Ridge, 1,200 feet, and other steep, strenuous sections.
Special attractions: Moose, high ridges, scenery, Feldmann Lake, Siskiwit Bay, Island Mine. Connects to the Greenstone Ridge Trail.
Best season: Summer.
For more information: Park Superintendent, Isle Royale National Park, 87 North Ripley Street, Houghton, MI 49931; Isle Royale *Queen* Ferry, Copper Harbor, MI 49918, (906) 482-4950.
Finding the trailhead: The trail begins and ends at the Windigo ferry dock on the west side of Isle Royale.

The hike: This 24-mile loop is a mildly rugged trail that traces the southwestern corner of the park, an area with few tough stretches and plenty of scenery. Most of the trek is along fairly level trails, but hikers should prepare for two tough sections over Greenstone and Feldmann ridges, with the latter being the toughest.

From Windigo, hikers head generally west and then south for a 9-mile hike to the campground at Feldmann Lake. The first 5.5 miles of the hike go through a marshy area frequented by the island's largest resident, the moose. The final few miles to campground provide occasional glimpses of Rainbow Cove. With 0.5 mile to go, hikers will catch sight of their destination.

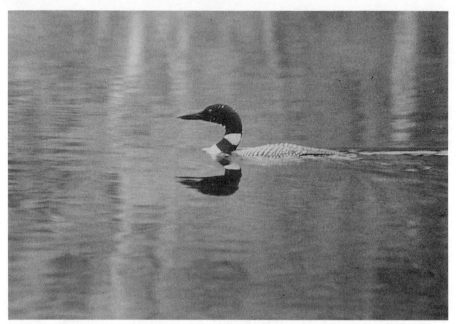

Human anglers aren't the only fishermen on these waters, as this loon prowls for a snack.

The trek from Feldmann Lake to Siskiwit Bay could be a hiker's toughest full day spent on the island. The 10.2-mile leg of this loop includes 5 miles of tough hiking along Feldmann Ridge. From the Feldmann Lake Campground, the first 1.5 miles spent ascending the ridge are typical of what is ahead—a steep rise that pretty much sets the pattern for the next 5 miles. An observation tower located about midway along the ridge is a welcome rest area; you are about halfway through the tough part of the ridge, and halfway through this tough section of the hike as well. Nearly 2 miles east of the tower you begin the long descent to Siskiwit Bay. After hiking this section, it's not at all uncommon to give in to the urge to linger for an extra day, especially knowing that a tough hike along the Greenstone Ridge is just a few miles north.

The short 4.8 miles to the junction with the Greenstone Ridge Trail is a walk through the mining history of Isle Royale. Hikers pass the remains of many of the buildings and, near the end, the signs of the mine that gives its name to the trail, Island Mine. Just after leaving the mine, hikers face a steep ascent to Red Oak Ridge, at an elevation of more than 1,200 feet. After a few more yards, the Island Mine Campground comes into view. Depending on their conditioning, hikers can either choose to stay here for the night, or immediately hike the 6.5 downhill miles along the Greenstone back to Windigo.

5   ROCK HARBOR TRAIL

General description: A popular, relatively comfortable two- or three-day trail, with scenic shoreline views and camping sites near inland lakes.
General location: Isle Royale National Park.
Maps: Isle Royale Topographic Map.
Degree of difficulty: Moderate.
Length: 13 miles.
Elevations: No significant elevations.
Special attractions: Shoreline vistas, Siskiwit mine site, Moskey Basin, Lake Richie.
Best season: Summer.
For more information: Park Superintendent, Isle Royale National Park, 87 North Ripley Street, Houghton, MI 49931; Isle Royale *Queen* Ferry, Copper Harbor, MI 49918, (906) 482-4950.
Finding the trailhead: Take the ferry to Rock Harbor, where the trail begins.

The hike: According to park officials, this trail is probably the most heavily used trail on the island. Experienced hikers could go its entire length in just a couple of days, but the few obstacles along the way would challenge the casual hiker.

The parts of the hike, like those of most other hikes on the island, are measured by the distances between possible campsites. The first stop at Three-Mile Campground should confuse no one when asking how far it is. This initial section is an easy-to-follow trail that can be somewhat treacherous after a rain.

The second day on the trail beings with a 4.4-mile hike to Daisy Farm Campground. This section is relatively easy and has the added bonus of providing some remarkable offshore scenery. About halfway along this leg hikers will pass what's left of the Siskiwit Mine. From the mine site, it's another 2 miles to the campground.

The third day, 4 miles of the Rock Harbor Trail, ends at Moskey Basin and its campground. The path follows the Daisy Farm Trail for 0.2 mile before the trails split. The Rock Harbor Trail continues on, following the terrain as it parallels the shoreline of Moskey Basin around to the campground.

From this point, the trail continues for nearly 2 miles to Lake Richie, where it ends.

6   INDIAN PORTAGE TRAIL

General description: A trail over a historic American Indian portage route from McCargoe Cove to Chippewa Harbor.
General location: Isle Royale National Park.
Maps: Isle Royale Topographic Map.
Degree of difficulty: Moderate.

Length: 11 miles.

Elevations: Some strenuous ascents, but no significant elevations.

Special attractions: Inland lakes, wilderness scenery.

Best season: Summer.

For more information: Park Superintendent, Isle Royale National Park, 87 North Ripley Street, Houghton, MI 49931; Isle Royale *Queen* Ferry, Copper Harbor, MI 49918, (906) 482-4950.

Finding the trailhead: The trail begins at McCargoe Cove Campground, at an intersection with the Minong Ridge Trail. It ends at Chippewa Harbor.

The hike: Islanders named this trail because of legendary use by American Indians to portage canoes along the route from Chippewa Harbor north to McCargoe Cove. The route traces portions of the shorelines of four inland lakes on its way to the sheltered waters of McCargoe Cove. Not a difficult hike, the trail has varied terrain that will slow many hikers. Allow for a long day to enjoy this 11-mile trail.

From the junction with the Minong Ridge Trail at the McCargoe Cove Campground, the trail heads south tracing the western shores of Chickenbone Lake till it joins the Greenstone Ridge Trail. Only the final 0.2 mile before the Greenstone junction presents any obstacles—and this is a steep climb.

From the Greenstone, the trail continues south around the western edges of Lakes Livermore and LeSage. Here, the trail switches and is routed around the eastern edge of Lake Richie. It then follows the course of the stream flowing out of the lake until it reaches Chippewa Harbor. There are several ascents along this leg of the trail, plus several marshy areas known to provide plenty of bugs during the season. From the mouth of the stream, at Chippewa Harbor Campground, to the end of the trail, is about 0.5 mile east.

7   HUGINNIN COVE LOOP

General description: A side loop from the Minong Ridge Trail to a picturesque shoreline campground.

General location: Isle Royale National Park.

Maps: Isle Royale Topographic Map.

Degree of difficulty: Easy to moderate.

Length: 6.5 miles.

Elevations: No significant elevations.

Special attractions: Moose, wildlife, scenery.

Best season: Summer.

For more information: Park Superintendent, Isle Royale National Park, 87 North Ripley Street, Houghton, MI 49931; Isle Royale *Queen* Ferry, Copper Harbor, MI 49918, (906) 482-4950.

Finding the trailhead: The loop trail branches off the Minong Ridge Trail near Washington Creek. Its destination and midpoint, the Huginnin Cove Campground, is an easy 3-hour hike from the ferry dock in Windigo.

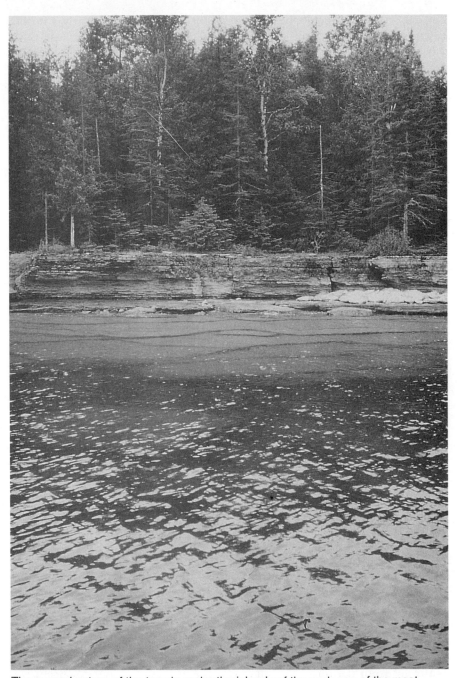

The rugged nature of the terrain make the islands of the park one of the most picturesque settings in the state.

The hike: This 6.5-mile loop is used as a warm up by hikers preparing for the rugged Minong Ridge Trail—the picturesque campground in Huginnin Cove is an easy 3-hour hike from the Windigo ferry, and makes a good first-night stopping place. The lowlands and swamps along this loop also provide hikers with an excellent opportunity to see moose and other wildlife.

The trail starts out on the Minong Ridge Trail. Hikers cross Washington Creek to reach the western trailhead for the loop several hundred yards after the creek crossing. The Huginnin trail heads generally north from the junction for 3.1 miles to the campground on the cove.

The hike back to the Minong Ridge Trail goes about 3.3 miles along the eastern half of the loop, following the Lake Superior shoreline briefly before turning south through a marshy area. The remains of several cabins and the ill-fated Windigo Mine community are still visible along the trail. From here, it is just yards to the junction with the Minong Ridge pathway.

8   ISHPEMING TRAIL

General description: A point-to-point trail between Malone Bay and Ishpeming Point.
General location: Isle Royale National Park.
Maps: Isle Royale Topographic Map.
Degree of difficulty: Moderate.
Length: 7 miles.
Elevations: Red Oak Ridge, 1,088 feet; a ridgetop at 1,123 feet; Ishpeming Point, 1,377 feet.
Special attractions: Connector to the Greenstone Ridge Trail; wilderness forest.
Best season: Summer.
For more information: Park Superintendent, Isle Royale National Park, 87 North Ripley Street, Houghton, MI 49931; Isle Royale *Queen* Ferry, Copper Harbor, MI 49918, (906) 482-4950.
Finding the trailhead: The trail begins at the ferry dock in Malone Bay, and ends on the Greenstone Ridge Trail at Ishpeming Point, or vice versa.

The hike: This 7-mile trail connects Malone Bay to the Greenstone Ridge Trail at Ishpeming Point. There are three steep climbs along the route, including the steepest climb of all—the trek to the peak of Ishpeming Point.

The trail can be hiked from the junction with the Greenstone (north to south), or from the ferry dock at Malone Bay (south to north). From the Greenstone trailhead, the hike is all downhill, but you have to rely on water transportation once you reach the end of the trail to get you to your next destination. The hike from south to north is more difficult, but allows more flexibility in planning connecting hikes.

From Malone Bay, the trail traces the southern shores of Siskiwit Lake for more than 3 miles before it turns decidedly north and begins to climb. The trail's first major ascent, to Red Oak Ridge, is a 1-mile rise to an elevation of 1,088 feet.

The next 2.5 miles are real knee-benders: a quick descent off Red Oak Ridge into a marshy lowland, followed quickly by a climb to the second ridgeline that tops out at 1,123 feet. After one more descent, it's a quick climb to Ishpeming Point. From the point, campgrounds are located at Lake Desor, to the west, and Hatchet Lake, to the east.

ADDITIONAL TRAILS

Stoll Trail—This easy 2-hour, 4.3-mile hike from the Rock Harbor Lodge traces the finger of rock east of the lodge, leading to Scoville Point. The trail is fairly level and poses no special problems for even the casual hiker. Hikers will get a great view of not only Lake Superior but also Tobin Harbor, and may even catch a glimpse of ancient copper mining sites near the lodge.

It is nearly 2 miles to Scoville Point from the lodge; the trail is easy to follow. The return trip requires retracing your steps for 0.5 mile, then heading along the southern edge of Tobin Harbor to get back to the lodge.

This trail offers a great after-dinner hike or just a chance to stretch your legs while you wait for the ferry back to the mainland.

Tobin Harbor Trail—This 3-mile linear route is an easy hike along the shoreline. It is an easy day hike from the lodge in Rock Harbor, or a good jumping-off point for longer treks, including the Greenstone. The trail is wide and easy to follow, offering no special problems for hikers at any level of experience. The short trail ends at the junction with the Mount Franklin Trail.

Hatchet Lake Trail—This 2.6-mile connector trail links Minong Ridge with the Greenstone Ridge Trail and provides access to the Hatchet Lake Campground. The short trail is not an easy trek, however, because of a moderate number of quick climbs and stream crossings, regardless of which end you choose to start.

From the Greenstone junction, the trails drops elevation quickly, reaching the shore of Hatchet Lake in about 0.3 mile. The trail curves east around the end of the lake before swinging back north to join the Minong Ridge Trail. This final half of the trail includes the roughest terrain and stream crossings. The campground at Todd Harbor is a bit under 1.5 miles east of the Minong Ridge Trail junction.

Lane Cove Trail—The Lane Cove Trail is a 2.5-mile spur trail to the Lane Cove Campground that offers hikers a respite from the Greenstone, or an alternate start to that long trek westward along the ridge. Either way, it is easily reached from the Greenstone Ridge Trail, just east of the summit of Mount Franklin, or from Rock Harbor by means of the Tobin Harbor and Mount Franklin trails.

From the junction with the Greenstone, the trail descends from the ridge and drops into a fairly wet area as it snakes north toward Lane Cove. The hike can be tough if the trail is wet, but a little caution along steeper sections will help. Hiking the 2.5 miles to the campground won't take longer than a couple of hours.

Mount Franklin Trail—Hikers using this 2-mile trail usually make their appearance from the south, at Three-Mile Campground, or from the east, on the Tobin Harbor Trail. Hikers coming the opposite direction, from the north, are generally winding up their west-to-east hike along the Greenstone and are bound for Rock Harbor and its ferry dock.

Leaving Three-Mile Campground, south-originating hikers will first go west for 0.15 mile to the junction with the Mount Franklin Trail, then north toward its junction with the Tobin Harbor Trail, about 0.5 mile later. The terrain in the area means lots of ups and downs—mostly ups. Waiting at the end of the hike is the climb to the crest of Greenstone Ridge, leaving the worst for last if you make the hike from the south.

The trail tops out just east of Mount Franklin and its 1,074-foot crest.

Daisy Farm Trail—The 2-mile Daisy Farm Trail is mentioned in the Greenstone Ridge Trail description; it is the western approach to the campground at the Greenstone's southern terminus at Rock Harbor. This spur trail provides relief from the rigors of the Greenstone, but by no means is rated an easy hike. This is due to the rough terrain leading to and from the campground. The scenery is great, but be prepared to do some climbing.

Ojibway Trail—The 1.7-mile Ojibway Trail is the eastern leg of the route followed by many hikers making their way back to the Greenstone from the Daisy Farm Campground. The return trail is still steep, but does not compare to the terrain along the Daisy Farm Trail to the west.

East Chickenbone Trail—This 1.6-mile trail is a unique mix of terrain and habitats, offering an alternate route to the Minong Ridge and Greenstone Ridge trails. It also provides a pathway around the eastern shores of Chickenbone Lake. The trail traces the eastern shores of the lake before heading cross-country to join the Indian Portage Trail for the trek to McCargoe Cove. The few brief climbs and descents here offer nothing overly challenging.

Windigo Nature Trail—The shortest trail on the island, this 1.2-mile nature hike follows a twelve-stop, self-guided route near the harbor at Windigo. A brochure available at the visitor center outlines each of the stops and provides all the information you need to enjoy this brief and scenic hike.

9-17   *PORCUPINE MOUNTAINS WILDERNESS STATE PARK*

Overview

Michigan's Porcupine Wilderness State Park is the largest of the state's parks, covering nearly 60,000 acres in Ontonagon and Gogebic counties. The park is one of the most visited in Michigan, but few visitors venture more than a few yards from their cars; most stay only long enough to snap a few photographs of the incredible vistas seen from scenic overlooks. Although a drive through the remote northern fringes of Michigan's Upper Peninsula sets the mood for a visit to this unique state park of virgin forest and undisturbed shoreline, there is only one way to see what this park has to offer—travel on foot!

Porcupine Mountains Wilderness State Park stretches 25 miles along southern Lake Superior, and inland for nearly 10 miles, to include four major lakes, numerous streams and rivers, and dozens of waterfalls, many unnamed. This remote area also contains one of the most extensive virgin hardwood forests east of the Rocky Mountains, as well as nearly every type of flora and fauna native to Michigan. The streams that feed Lake Superior host large schools of spawning salmon and steelhead each fall.

Hiking along the Presque Isle River Trail. Michigan DNR, Parks and Recreation Division photo.

This rugged region of the Upper Peninsula offers both mountain challenge and Great Lakes beauty in its more than 90 miles of trails. The trail system in Porcupine Mountains Wilderness State Park allows hikers the opportunity to match skill and experience with their available time to create the perfect outdoor adventure. Trails lengths vary considerably, from the 16-mile Lake Superior Trail, which extends along the shoreline of its namesake, to the 0.75-mile Greenstone Falls Access Trail. The park visitor center can provide an updated trail map that also locates camping possibilities in the park, designed specifically to compliment USGS maps.

Hikes through the Porcupine Mountains are rated moderate to difficult, leaning toward the high end of the scale because of rugged and often remote terrain. This is not an area for the casual hiker; inexperienced hikers are cautioned to solicit the assistance of experienced hikers or, as one local hiker advised, "Take it in small bites!" Good, solid footwear is a must if you plan to venture far beyond the parking lot. The trails themselves are not easily traversed in many areas because of uneven, rocky terrain that is "booby-trapped" with roots from trailside trees and stretches of coarse sand. Be prepared for all conditions, and do not take the region lightly.

Elevations in the Porcupines range from the sublime shoreline of Lake Superior to severe heights as hikers climb 1,958-foot Summit Peak. The most prominent site in the park is the Lake of the Clouds Overlook, offering easy access and a stunning view of the park's rugged interior. A second, less accessible overlook is the Summit Peak Tower, which looks out at the scenic Superior shoreline.

Throughout the park, remnants of a once-active copper industry can be found, marked by a few posts and beams. More than three dozen mines are scattered throughout the park; hikers should be aware of the potential hazards these areas pose. The park's wilderness is framed by towering pines, hundreds of years old, which escaped the saw. Loggers were allowed into one small section of the park following a major storm, but there are few other reminders of the rich logging history of northern Michigan within park confines.

The park is generally free of snow and ice from May through October, but the prime season to visit the park is during fall, when the Porcupine Mountains are colored by the season. The park is used by deer and small game hunters, so hikers are cautioned to wear bright clothing in the park after September 15. Visiting the park immediately after the snow and ice have melted can be an especially quiet time in this vast wilderness—and cold, too—but waiting until the weather warms will expose hikers to squadrons of flying, biting insects such as black flies, no-see-ums, mosquitos, deer flies, and gnats.

Trailheads for many of the park's twenty-two trails are located at junctions with other pathways through the interior region of this wilderness area and, as such, create a web of possible loops. Each trail described in this book is treated separately rather than as part of a complete loop; the trail descriptions include notations on intersections and junctions with other pathways in the Porcupines. This approach is meant to give hikers more flexibility in planning a trip in the region. Putting together a hike to match hikers' abilities and time-

9-17 PORCUPINE MOUNTAINS WILDERNESS STATE PARK

tables should require little more skill than it takes to assemble a peanut butter sandwich.

To reach the park, head to the western Upper Peninsula. The east end of the park is 10 miles north of Bergland on Michigan Highway 64, and 14 miles from Ontonagon along the shores of Lake Superior on Michigan Highway 107. The west entrance to the park is 16 miles from Wakefield, on County Road 519.

---

9   LAKE SUPERIOR TRAIL

General description: A point-to-point trail across the park along the shore of beautiful Lake Superior.

General location: Porcupine Mountains Wilderness State Park.

Maps: USGS Thomaston, White Pine, and Carp River quads; updated trail map available at the park's visitor center.

Degree of difficulty: Moderate to difficult.

Length: 16 miles.

Elevations: No significant elevations.

Special attractions: Waterfalls, Lake Superior shoreline, Presque Isle River.

Best season: Fall.

For more information: Park Manager, Porcupine Mountains Wilderness State Park, 599 Michigan Highway 107, Ontonagon, MI 49953, (906) 885-5275.

Finding the trailhead: Hikers starting at the eastern end of the trail begin at the trailhead about 1 mile east of the parking lot for the Lake of the Clouds Overlook. The trailhead is well marked on the north side of M-107. The entry point for the west trailhead is at the Presque Isle Campground at the end of County Road 519.

The hike: The longest trail in the park, the Lake Superior Trail is a point-to-point trail that runs nearly the full width of this wilderness area. Unless you have pre-positioned a second vehicle or made other arrangements to get back to your start point, you have no other option than to do an about-face and hike back. The most practical route for hikers along this trail that shadows the Lake Superior shoreline is to hike into the sunset, east to west. That way, once you have descended from the Escarpment Overlook, the rest of the hike is downhill.

The first 2 miles of trail from the trailhead off M-107 head generally north to the "bottom of the hill" and the first approach to the shoreline of Lake Superior. Near the shore, hikers will reach the first manmade shelter along this 16-mile trail, Buckshot Cabin, just a few hundred yards ahead after you hit the bottom of the descent. It is nearly 7 miles to the next shelter (other than one you can carry in your backpack), so those who need rest should pause here.

For the next 3 miles, the trail plays hide-and-seek with the shoreline of Lake Superior, often screened from sight but loud with the sound of pounding waves. The first marked junction in the trail comes next, showing the way to a spot called Lone Rock, a huge glacial remnant. This is a good spot to set up a tent and allow those knees to recover from the earlier descent to the lakeshore. About 1 mile further down the trail, hikers will find an Adirondack shelter. Hikers looking for a roof over their heads might want to check in here, since this will be the last such shelter for nearly 3 miles.

From the shelter it's an easy hike to the mouth of the Big Carp River and the first junction with another major trail on the east bank, the Big Carp River Trail (see Hike 10). Past the junction, a short wooden bridge provides access to the west bank of the river. Once across the bridge, hikers will find the posted junction with the next trail, the Cross Trail (Hike 16). Just a stone's throw from the junction is another cabin, the Big Carp River Cabin. If hikers follow the set of steps to the campground named after the nearby river, a second cabin, the Lake Superior Cabin, is just a few short yards away. A possible side trip from this point would be an easy 1-mile hike to Shining Cloud Falls, the highest waterfall in the park.

About 0.5 mile west of the campground, a bridge provides access over Toledo Creek. About 1 mile farther is the next major junction, the northern start point for the Little Carp River Trail. Hikers will find a prepared campsite on the east bank of the river. After crossing the river, you reach the west bank of the river and a short spur trail to the Little Carp River Cabin "climbing about a million stairs!" Here also is the next trail junction, the northern trailhead for the Pinkerton Trail (Hike 15).

Crossing the Little Carp River along the Beaver Creek Trail. Michigan DNR, Parks and Recreation Division photo.

After passing the junction, hikers will find it is a quick 0.5 mile to Pinkerton Creek. The creek crossing is made tough by a 60-foot deep ravine guarding the flanks of this waterway. You are only about 6 miles from the end of the Lake Superior Trail, but face some of the toughest terrain found anywhere along its length. Still, if it's scenery you want, this is the place to be. Before the trail's end, you'll cross three small creeks without the aid of bridges; rock-hoppers will be able to keep their boots dry.

Hikers will reach a junction with a short spur trail leading to Speakers Cabin, which is nearly 0.5 mile from the main trail. At the junction, hikers have about 2 miles left on the Lake Superior Trail. The terrain separating hikers from here to the Presque Isle Campground is rocky and punctuated by ravines. The final barrier, the Presque Isle River, is Michigan's premier whitewater river, but bridges and boardwalks will make the crossing a dry one.

On the east bank of the river hikers will pass the junction with the East River Trail, one half of the loop trail that flanks the Presque Isle River and provides campers a chance to "get lost" in the wilderness of the mountains (see Additional Hikes). A steep descent to a swing bridge over the river, a steep climb to the top of the ravine carved by the waterway, a pause to take in the beauty of the last landmark on the Lake Superior Trail, and—it's over!

10   LITTLE AND BIG CARP RIVER TRAILS

General description: Hikes along two of the park's rivers, between uplands and shore.
General location: Porcupine Mountains Wilderness State Park.
Maps: USGS Thomaston, White Pine, and Carp River quads; an updated trail map is available at the park's visitor center.
Degree of difficulty: Moderate, and at times easy.
Length: Little Carp River Trail, 11 miles; Big Carp River Trail, 9 miles.
Elevations: The Little Carp River Trail climbs to 1,600 feet.
Special attractions: Waterfalls, streams, Lake Superior shore. These trails are ideal segments of larger trail loops from shore to uplands, or vice versa.
Best season: Fall.
For more information: Park Manager, Porcupine Mountains Wilderness State Park, 599 Michigan Highway 107, Ontonagon, MI 49953, (906) 885-5275.
Finding the trailheads: The Little Carp River trail is an interior trail, beginning on its northern end at a well-marked junction with the Lake Superior Trail on the east side of the Little Carp River; to reach it, hike 6 miles east from the Presque Isle River along the Lake Superior Trail. The southern end of the trail begins at Mirror Lake. The Big Carp River trail begins at the end of the parking lot for the Lake of the Clouds Overlook, at the end of M-107, and ends on the Lake Superior Trail and shore.
The hikes: Little Carp River Trail—From the trail's junction with the Lake

Superior Trail, hikers will lose elevation as they make the trek to the bed of the Little Carp River. This will be the first of many ups and downs along this trail; the route gains nearly 1,000 feet in elevation from trailhead to trailhead.

Within the next 2 miles hikers will make a number of stream crossings, all without the aid of bridges. About 0.5 mile later, the first of two waterfalls, Explorer Falls, comes into view. The next, Trapper Falls, comes several hundred yards farther down the trail. From the falls, the trail is fairly easy to negotiate and follows the trace of the river. It begins to get a bit steeper as it makes a turn northwest, heading for its terminus at Mirror Lake.

About 6 miles after leaving Lake Superior, hikers will reach the Cross Trail and a short trail that leads to the Greenstone Falls Cabin. Several hundred yards farther, hikers will meet the access trail to Little Carp River Road, to the south. The trail continues its trace toward Mirror Lake, eventually climbing to an elevation of nearly 1,600 feet before it meets up with the Lily Pond trailhead, on the south (right) side of the main trail. The next 3 miles are a "walk in the park," according to park officials, compared to previous trail miles. The next trail junction is found about 1 mile later, when the Little Carp route meets the Beaver Creek Trail.

Just before reaching Mirror Lake, hikers will reach the South Mirror Lake Trail and, a few yards later, the Correction Line Trail. Continue on the Little Carp River trail, which ends on the northwest corner of the lake.

Big Carp River Trail—This trail runs east-west through the park from the Lake of the Clouds Overlook to the Lake Superior Trail at the mouth of the Big Carp River. The first 2 miles of trail carry hikers from the overlook's rugged beauty and the height of the escarpment down into the valley of the Big Carp River. It is quite a drop in elevation, but not a difficult hike.

At the bottom, the hike through the river valley is actually quite enjoyable and fairly easy. Nearly 4 miles along, hikers cross the river for the first time with the aid of a footbridge and then reach a junction with the Correction Line Trail. From here, the trail climbs out of the valley for about 1.5 miles before dropping back down so hikers can cross the river once again. After making the crossing, hikers climb once again out of the river valley and into a heavily forested area for a 2-mile hike to Shining Cloud Falls. From the falls, hikers drop back down to the river, following the trace to its rendezvous with Lake Superior.

11   GOVERNMENT PEAK TRAIL

General description: A trail from Escarpment Overlook to Mirror Lake along the Upper Carp River.
General location: Porcupine Mountains Wilderness State Park.
Maps: USGS Thomaston, White Pine, and Carp River quads; an updated trail map is available at the park's visitor center.
Degree of difficulty: Moderate.
Length: 7.5 miles.

Elevations: The trail gets steep as it rises toward the summit of Government Peak.

Special attractions: Upper Carp River, Government Peak, Mirror Lake.

Best season: Fall.

For more information: Park Manager, Porcupine Mountains Wilderness State Park, 599 Michigan Highway 107, Ontonagon, MI 49953, (906) 885-5275.

Finding the trailheads: The northern trailhead is 0.4 mile east of Escarpment Overlook, on the south side of the road. The western trailhead is the junction with the North Mirror Lake Trail, about 1 mile east of the lake.

The hike: From the north trailhead, 0.4 mile east of the parking lot for the Escarpment Overlook, hikers head south along the trail and quickly encounter three junctions with other trails. Within about 1 mile hikers pass the east end of the Escarpment Trail (Hike 17) and then both ends of the 3-mile Overlook Trail loop.

The first crossing of the Upper Carp River is next, about 1 mile from the trailhead. For the next mile, hikers are shadowed by the river as they head for the junction with the Union Spring Trail. Within the next mile, Trap Falls comes into view before another crossing of the Upper Carp must be negotiated.

Next is a junction with another major trail, the Lost Lake Trail. From this junction, the main pathway swings west. In 2 miles hikers will reach the headwaters of the Upper Carp River, where the trail begins to steepen as it rises toward the summit of Government Peak. As quickly as it rose, the trail drops down the west side of the peak and heads off for the final 2 miles to Mirror Lake. Nearly 0.5 mile from the lake, hikers will reach the junction with the North Mirror Lake Trail and the official end of the Government Peak Trail. If you intend to finish your day on the shores of Mirror Lake, you will have to go the short distance on a portion of the North Mirror Lake Trail to do so.

12   LOST LAKE TRAIL

General description: A scenic trail through wild forest to an inland lake and coldwater river.

General location: Porcupine Mountains Wilderness State Park.

Maps: USGS Thomaston, White Pine, and Carp River quads; an updated trail map is available at the park's visitor center.

Degree of difficulty: Moderate.

Length: 4.5 miles.

Elevations: High point of 1,500 feet.

Special attractions: Wilderness forest, Lake Superior views, Lost Lake, Upper Carp River.

Best season: Fall.

For more information: Park Manager, Porcupine Mountains Wilderness State Park, 599 Michigan Highway 107, Ontonagon, MI 49953, (906) 885-5275.

Bridges throughout the park keep hikers high and dry. Michigan DNR, Parks and Recreation Division photo.

Finding the trailheads: The southern Lost Lake trailhead is located along South Boundary Road, 7 miles from the M-107 junction. The start point is across the road from the Lost Creek Outpost Campground. The northern trailhead is at the trail's junction with the Government Peak Trail.

The hike: From the southern trailhead, the first 0.5 mile of the trail passes through a forested area but quickly climbs along a rocky pathway to the shoulder of Lost Creek. For about 1.5 miles from the trailhead, hikers will begin a steady ascent to reach an elevation of just over 1,500 feet. As you reach the high point of the trail near Lost Lake, the immense conifers provide a setting that is cathedral-like. With this, take in an equally picturesque view of the lake.

The trail then passes along the southern shore of Lost Lake and then around the western edge before assuming a northern course. Hikers leaving the shoreline of the lake should be prepared for a steep descent: you lose more than 200 feet in elevation in a quick 0.5 mile. Less than 1 mile from the lake hikers will have to wade the cold waters of the Upper Carp River. There is no bridge here, but the crossing can provide welcome relief from the hardness of the trail.

For the final 1.5 miles, hikers make a slow climb to the junction with the Government Peak Trail.

13 CORRECTION LINE TRAIL

General description: A connecting trail between the Big Carp River and Mirror Lake or the Little Carp River.
General location: Porcupine Mountains Wilderness State Park.
Maps: USGS Thomaston, White Pine, and Carp River quads; an updated trail map is available at the park's visitor center.
Degree of difficulty: Moderate.
Length: 3 miles.
Elevations: 1,600 feet at the overlook above Mirror Lake.
Special attractions: Big Carp River, Mirror Lake.
Best season: Fall.
For more information: Park Manager, Porcupine Mountains Wilderness State Park, 599 Michigan Highway 107, Ontonagon, MI 49953, (906) 885-5275.
Finding the trailhead: The Correction Line Trail is another of the interior park trails that can only be accessed from one of the other trails. The trailheads for this trail are located at a junction with the Big Carp River Trail, approximately 4 miles from Lake Superior, and at a posted junction with the North Mirror Lake Trail, on the north shore of Mirror Lake, nearly 5 miles from Lake of the Clouds.

The hike: Begin at the west trailhead, at a junction with the Big Carp River Trail, on the east shore of the Big Carp River (see Hike 10). The first 1 mile of the Correction Line Trail crosses very wet ground as the trail moves away from the river. Hikers won't leave the soggy footing behind until they cross Landlookers Creek. The area remains wet much of the year, making for an unavoidable sloppy start.

Once across the creek, hikers will make a slow ascent of nearly 2 miles. At first the climb is easy, but it quickens and does not get easier until hikers top out at a point nearly 1,600 feet high overlooking Mirror Lake. It is only a few hundred yards downhill to the lake and the end of this trail. At the final junction, the Little Carp River Trail heads west, and the North Mirror Lake Trail heads east.

14 MIRROR LAKE TRAILS

General description: Connector trails near Mirror Lake.
General location: Porcupine Mountains Wilderness State Park.
Maps: USGS Thomaston, White Pine, and Carp River quads; an updated trail map is available at the park's visitor center.
Degree of difficulty: Easy to moderate, with some stream crossings.
Length: North Mirror Lake Trail, 6.5 miles; South Mirror Lake Trail, 2.5 miles.
Elevations: Some ascents of more than 200 feet.

Special attractions: Mirror Lake, Lake of the Clouds.

Best season: Fall.

For more information: Park Manager, Porcupine Mountains Wilderness State Park, 599 Michigan Highway 107, Ontonagon, MI 49953, (906) 885-5275.

Finding the trailheads: The North Mirror Lake Trail begins at Mirror Lake itself; it ends at the end of the parking lot for the Lake of the Clouds Overlook. The South Mirror Lake trailhead is at the end of Summit Peak Road, about 1.5 miles from South Boundary Road.

The hikes: North Mirror Lake Trail—From the trailhead on the north shore of Mirror Lake, this trail heads north toward Lake of the Clouds, 4 miles away. The first mile is considered easy, but it also requires that hikers cross a moderate number of small streams before reaching a junction with the Government Peak Trail.

From the junction, the next 2.5 miles of this trail are a series of gentle climbs and steep drops to the ridges overlooking Lake of the Clouds. The long drop to the bottom of a ridge to cross Scott Creek is the final marker before you reach the lake. From the western edge of the lake, the trail turns right to follow the north shore before it climbs to the parking lot for the overlook. Hikers will climb nearly 200 feet from the lake before reaching the end of the trail.

South Mirror Lake Trail—From the trailhead on Summit Peak Road, this 2.5-mile trail heads north to the western shore of Mirror Lake. The trail is easy to follow, but involves a series of major ups and downs, several of them rising or falling 200 feet or more. Just over 1 mile from the trailhead, hikers will reach a junction with the Summit Peak Trail. In another mile, hikers must cross the Little Carp River to reach a junction with the Little Carp River Trail. The next junction will be with the Correction Line Trail. The final few hundred yards of the trail are along the north shore of Mirror Lake, continuing to a point where the southern trail merges into the North Mirror Lake Trail.

---

15   *PINKERTON CREEK TRAIL*

General description: A brief and pleasant connector trail to or from the Little Carp River.

General location: Porcupine Mountains Wilderness State Park.

Maps: USGS Thomaston, White Pine, and Carp River quads; an updated trail map is available at the park's visitor center.

Degree of difficulty: Easy.

Length: 3 miles.

Elevations: No significant elevations.

Special attractions: Many hikers use this trail to bypass the rugged end of the west-to-east Lake Superior Trail, which goes from the Presque Isle River to the Little Carp River.

Best season: Fall.

The bridge over the Big Carp River along the North Mirror Lake Trail. Michigan DNR, Parks and Recreation Division photo.

For more information: Park Manager, Porcupine Mountains Wilderness State Park, 599 Michigan Highway 107, Ontonagon, MI 49953, (906) 885-5275.
Finding the trailheads: The well-marked southern trailhead is located along South Boundary Road, about 20 miles west of the park's visitor center and about 5 miles east of Presque Isle Campground. The northern trailhead is where the Pinkerton Creek Trail intersects the Lake Superior Trail, 5.5 miles east of the Presque Isle River.

The hike: From the southern trailhead, the first mile of trail leads through mature hardwood stands before it reaches its namesake, Pinkerton Creek. A wooden bridge allows for a dry-foot crossing; within a few yards, a second, smaller creek and another handy bridge have to be crossed as you hike through stands of ancient hardwoods and conifers. With less than 0.5 mile to go to the end of the trail, hikers break out on the west bank of the Little Carp River and shadow the river for the final few hundred yards to the shore of Lake Superior.

16 CROSS TRAIL

General description: A connector trail between two of the park's major trails.
General location: Porcupine Mountains Wilderness State Park.
Maps: USGS Thomaston, White Pine and Carp River quads; an updated trail map is available at the park's visitor center.

Degree of difficulty: Moderate.

Length: 5 miles.

Elevations: No significant elevations.

Special attractions: Big Carp River, swamp ecology, connector trail possibilities.

Best season: Fall, when bugs are less active.

For more information: Park Manager, Porcupine Mountains Wilderness State Park, 599 Michigan Highway 107, Ontonagon, MI 49953, (906) 885-5275.

Finding the trailheads: The southern trailhead is at a junction with the Little Carp Trail, 5.5 miles south of the Lake Superior shoreline and west of Greenstone Falls, on the north bank of the Little Carp River. Another southern entry to the trail is possible from a parking lot along South Boundary Road, near the junction with Little Carp River Road. The distance from the parking area to the trailhead is about 0.5 mile. The northern trailhead is at a junction with the Lake Superior Trail at the mouth of the Big Carp River.

The hike: From the southern trailhead on the Little Carp Trail hikers go 0.5 mile before dropping into an extensive wet area known as the Memengwa Swamp. The wetlands can be especially buggy early in the hiking season, and will be challenging regardless of the time of the year you visit. After 1.5 trail miles, the swamp turns into a relatively dry forest as hikers begin to climb out of the wet basin. A slight climb over the next mile of the trail ends at an overlook that presents the first look at the Big Carp River.

From here, the trail drops quickly over a short distance, losing nearly 100 feet of elevation. Hikers are within 0.5 mile of the Lake Superior Trail as they pass Bathtub Falls, the final adjustment in elevation made by the Big Carp River as it spills toward Lake Superior. The end of the trail comes quickly. The trailhead on the Lake Superior Trail is on the west side of the river.

---

17   ESCARPMENT TRAIL

General description: A linear trail with scenic views of Lake of the Clouds.

General location: Porcupine Mountains Wilderness State Park.

Maps: USGS Thomaston, White Pine, and Carp River quads; an updated trail map is available at the park's visitor center.

Degree of difficulty: Moderate.

Length: 4 miles.

Elevations: Ascents to Cloud Peak and Cuyahoga Peak.

Special attractions: Lake of the Clouds views; Carp Lake Mine; Cuyahoga Mine.

Best season: Fall.

For more information: Park Manager, Porcupine Mountains Wilderness State Park, 599 Michigan Highway 107, Ontonagon, MI 49953, (906) 885-5275.

Finding the trailhead: The trailhead is also the same one at the Lake of the Clouds Overlook used by hikers walking the North Mirror Lake Trail, but the Escarpment Trail turns southeast 0.5 mile after starting the trek.

The hike: This point-to-point trail offers a unique view of the most scenic point in the park, Lake of the Clouds. A spur trail about midway between Cloud Peak and Cuyahoga Peak divides the trail in half.

Leaving the Lake of the Clouds Overlook, hikers actually start the trek on North Mirror Lake Trail, heading south for nearly 0.5 mile before breaking away on the Escarpment Trail. From the junction, the path swings east. Hikers will start climbing as they head for the first landmark, Cloud Peak. At the peak, hikers will enjoy a look at the east end of Lake of the Clouds, something few visitors get to enjoy. After a quick drop off the east side of the peak, hikers will reach the junction to a shortcut spur leading north back to M-107. Hikers are now at the halfway point of the trail.

Continuing east, the next landmark, the Carp Lake Mine, is reached just prior to the start of the climb to Cuyahoga Peak. The trail passes the actual summit and starts a long descent to the eastern trailhead, passing the Cuyahoga Mine about 400 yards from the junction with the Government Peak Trail.

Turn north (left) at the junction for a 300-yard hike back to M-107.

ADDITIONAL TRAILS

Overlook Trail Loop—The 3.5-mile Overlook Trail shares a trailhead with the Government Peak Trail, but for less than 0.5 mile. The short loop actually traces a portion of the longer Government Peak Trail to return to the parking lot on M-107. This loop is one of the few actual round-trip hikes in the park.

The first 2 miles of this day hike are easy, but hikers will then climb steadily to a point just over 1,500 feet in elevation. After the climb, the remaining 1.5 miles are downhill to the junction with the Government Peak Trail. You will lose more than 350 feet from the trail's high point before you reach the southern junction.

Once you reach the junction, turn back north (left) for the 0.7-mile hike back to the M-107 trailhead.

Whitetail Path—The trailhead is located on the south side of M-107, near the Union Bay Campground. This 1-mile trail is a spur trail, offering a level, easy hike used primarily by campers from Union Bay Campground. It provides access to the park's interpretive center.

Visitor Center Nature Trail—This nature trail starts at the rear of the visitor center. The trail is one of two nature trails at the east end of the park. The 1-mile loop is punctuated by a number of stations describing flora of the area. It connects to the Whitetail Path for just a few yards before returning to the visitor center.

Union Mine Trail—The trailhead for this 1-mile trail is approximately 2 miles south of the park's headquarters and the M-107 junction on South Boundary Road. Signposts along this interpretive route permit hikers a choice of directions; the trail shadows the Union and Little Union rivers. It is a brief but miniature view of the interior of the park, revealing a glimpse into the past of the mining activity of the region.

Union Spring Trail—The eastern trailhead for this trail is several hundred yards south of the Union Mine Trail trailhead; the western end of the trail is the junction with Government Peak Trail, 4 miles away. This easy, nearly level trail offers an alternative way to reach the Government Peak Trail, bypassing the more rugged start on the trek to Mirror Lake.

Leaving the trailhead off South Boundary Road, hikers move along an ancient two-track for nearly 0.6 mile. A gate blocks potential vehicular access; beyond that point, the trail heads west into the heart of the park. The trail crosses the Union River, heading west, and Union Spring. A somewhat confusing junction appears next, and park officials warn hikers to be ready for it. About 1 mile from the trailhead, the trail and a grown-over two-track come together. The trail heads west and the roadway turns off to the northwest.

Several hundred yards from this junction, Union Spring appears. The spring is the halfway mark in the trail. The trail's remaining 2 miles continue west through a marshy area and then go up a bit to dry out for the final mile to the junction with the Government Peak Trail.

At trail's end, hikers have three choices: do an about-face and retrace their steps to the starting point; turn right and head for M-107, about 2 miles north; or turn left and continue on the Government Peak Trail.

Summit Peak Tower Trail—The trailhead for this short trail is located at the end of the parking lot at the end of Summit Peak Road. The 800 yards from the trailhead to the tower and platform atop Summit Peak are an easy hike and offer a chance to view the park's interior. The trail is easy to follow, and the ascent to the summit is not difficult. If you want to continue on this trail and link up with the South Mirror Lake Trail, you need to be aware that the remaining 0.5 mile of the trail is not going to be easy. The steep descent down the north side of the peak prompts most visitors to simply retrace their steps to Summit Peak Road.

Beaver Creek Trail—The starting point for this 2-mile trail is the same as for the Summit Peak Tower Trail, but this trail swings west out of the parking lot. This trail is another of the short access trails used to reach the Little Carp River Trail. From the trailhead at the end of Summit Peak Road it is a quick mile to the trail's junction with the Little Carp, an easy path into the interior of the park with no major obstacles along the way.

Lily Pond Trail—The eastern trailhead for the 3-mile Lily Pond Trail is found approximately 0.75 mile up Summit Peak Road from its junction with South Boundary Road. The western end of the trail is 3 miles away, at the trail's junction with the Little Carp River Trail. From the trailhead on Summit Peak

Road, hikers will have to make a gentle climb to the high point on the trail, at just over 1,700 feet elevation.

Greenstone Falls Access Trail—Hikers will find the trailhead for this 0.75-mile trail at the end of Little Carp River Road, 16 miles from the visitor center. The trail follows the Little Carp River until reaching a designated crossing point near the end of the 1,000-yard trail. Once across the river, hikers make an easy climb to the opposite shoulder and the junction with the Little Carp River Trail.

East & West River Loop—The trailheads for the two trails that make up this loop are both located at the eastern edge of the Presque Isle Campground Day-Use Area. The trails form a 2-mile loop along the flanks of the Presque Isle River, a waterway considered the premier whitewater stream in the state. Hikers descend along the gorge created by the river to cross a swing bridge before climbing back out to reach the actual start of the East River Trail. Turning south, hikers will next encounter two major waterfalls—the Manabezho and the Manido—within the first 0.5 mile of trail. Several hundred yards ahead, the final waterfall, the Nawadaha, signals the final steps of the trail. Hikers will end the East River Trail on South Boundary Road, on the east end of the bridge.

A quick few steps across the bridge and hikers will step onto the West River Trail, the second half of the trek, and go along the Presque Isle River. This half of the loop is easier to negotiate than the first mile, and retraces many of the same sights seen earlier including the three major waterfalls. As quickly as it began, the hike is completed as hikers climb out to the trailhead in the Presque Isle Campground.

18   *SYLVANIA WILDERNESS & RECREATION AREA*

Overview

The Sylvania Wilderness and Recreation Area is an 18,327-acre step back to a quieter time in northern Michigan. This large natural area comes complete with old-growth forest and pristine lakes, providing habitat for all sorts of plants and creatures. Wildflowers of all sorts, even rare orchids, can be found throughout the area. Migrating waterfowl, loons, eagles, and osprey are common sights around many of the lakes in the tract. Deer, bear, and birds of all sorts inhabit the area, while trophy-class smallmouth bass abound in many of the lakes along with walleye, northern pike, and pan fish. About 20 miles of trails wind through the area, connecting most of its thirty-six named lakes like dots in a puzzle.

The area was purchased in 1895 by a Wisconsin-based lumber man who intended to cut its ancient red and white pines but changed his mind once he

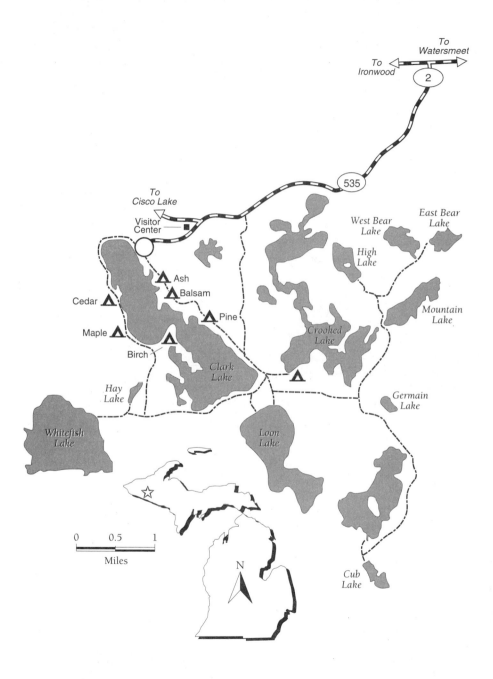

saw the area around Clark Lake. Friends joined him in preserving the beauty of the Sylvania tract and formed the Sylvania Club, and fishing and hunting replaced the activities of ax and saw. In 1967 the USDA Forest Service purchased the land and opened it to the public. In 1987 the Sylvania tract was designated a federal wilderness area, following passage of the Michigan Wilderness Act.

The wilderness area offers pristine beauty along with solitude—and a quiet insured by a ban on motorized boats and vehicles. Designated campsites help keep the area as it was at the turn of the century. Special regulations control the use of the area and fishing within it, but the extra efforts they require pale by comparison with the wilderness they preserve.

Only one of the trails through the Sylvania tract can be considered an actual loop, and that is the 7-mile loop around Clark Lake. But spur trails that can be used to create a walk through the wilderness that will take hikers deep into the nearly 19,000 acres of tangles and watery wonderland that make up this area. The trails are all marked with bright blue blazes and are wide and easily traveled; many were two-track roads into private cabin sites at the turn of the century. Of all the campsites around the thirty-six lakes in the area, only about half can be reached via the trail systems. The remainder require a canoe to reach.

Regardless of which trail system you choose to explore, it becomes evident very quickly as to why favorite trails are nearest to the lakeshore: mosquitos. The area's inland trails are tough to enjoy in late May and early June because of the presence of these needle-nosed pests and their bloodsucking colleagues, black flies. It doesn't take a rocket scientist to figure out why campsites are adjacent to the lakes.

Special Notes: Between May 15 and September 30, every overnight camper needs to have a validated overnight camping permit, and day users must have a day use permit. Assignments of campsites will be done on a first-come, first-served basis. Camping reservations must be made with the Sylvania Visitors Center at least fourteen days in advance. Day use permits, obtained at the entrance station, cannot be reserved.

Wilderness users can make reservations by mail; these are accepted starting on January 15 of each year. To reserve a spot, campers must mail an application along with a $5 non-refundable fee per reservation to the Sylvania Visitor Center, P.O. Box 276, Watersmeet, MI 49969. Starting February 1, telephone reservations may be made by calling (906) 358-4724 or (906) 358-4834 during the following times: February 1 - May 14, 7:30 a.m. - 4 p.m., Monday through Friday; May 15 - Sept. 30, 9 a.m. - 5 p.m., seven days a week. If you are given a campsite reservation by phone, your $5 reservation fee must reach the center within seven days for confirmation.

The permit you receive must be validated at the park entrance when you arrive, before you hit the trail. No check-out is required, but you are asked to vacate your campsite by 2 p.m. on the day the permit expires. A complete packet of information including special regulations regarding use of the area and the restrictive fishing rules will be sent along with your permit package.

Use permits are not required at any other time of the year, but hikers must self-register at visitor stations in the park. There are special fishing restrictions governing size and possession limits, so be sure to check before keeping any fish.

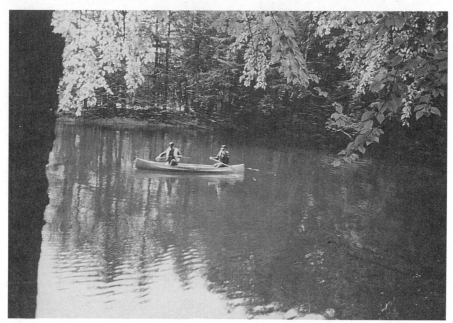
Fishermen are the prime users of the Sylvania's bounty, but hikers will also encounter hunters each fall.

General description: Trails in wilderness and an adjoining recreation area of nearly 19,000 acres.

General location: The western end of the Upper Peninsula, about 10 miles west of Watersmeet, along the Michigan-Wisconsin border.

Maps: Maps are available from the information centers operated by the Forest Service; trails are well marked.

Degree of difficulty: Easy to moderate, depending on length, with trails generally clear of debris.

Length: 20 miles on various trails in the area. By looping along connecting trails to the three dozen lakes in the Sylvania area, hikers can customize their visits.

Elevations: Flat with a few minor rises; these are gentle and require no excessive effort.

Special attractions: 36 lakes surrounded by old-growth forest with stands of virgin red and white pines; wildflowers; waterfowl; excellent fishing. The sense of wilderness, however, is perhaps the most special of all attractions of the Sylvania area.

Best season: Summer and after. Trails are accessible after the snow melts in late April or early May, but hikers would be advised to wait until mid-June—wait, that is, for the black fly population to ebb just a bit. Some outstanding scenery unfolds in the fall, but hikers must be aware that hunters use this area extensively for small game and deer hunting from mid-September until snow blocks access.

For more information: Sylvania Wilderness Visitor Center, P.O. Box 276, Watersmeet, MI 49969, (906) 358-4724; Watersmeet Ranger Station, Watersmeet, MI 49969, (906) 358-4551; Gogebic Area Convention & Visitor Bureau, 126 West Arch, Ironwood, MI 49938, (906) 932-4850.

Finding the trailhead: The Clark Lake trailhead is the best starting point for the Sylvania trail system. It is located near the lakeshore of Clark Lake at the end of the parking lot for the boat launch. Signs from the visitor information center off County Road 535 will direct you to the site.

The hikes: The 7-mile loop around Clark Lake starts just off the parking lot about 1 mile from the visitor center. If getting away from it all is one of the reasons you hike in the first place, take the trail to the northwest (left) as you are standing at the lakeshore. Going in this direction will require a 1.5-mile hike to the first campsite, Cedar. The trail is even and easy, and by the time you reach the camp you will be on the opposite shore of Clark Lake. There are three campsites on the western shore: Maple is about 0.5 mile from Cedar, and Birch is nearly 0.75 mile from Maple, tucked in a protected little bay near the southern end of the lake.

From the Birch campsite, the trail swings directly south and into the bugs, away from the open shoreline for nearly 1 mile. About halfway along this section of trail, hikers will cross the portage between Glimmerglass and Hay lakes. ("Portage," by the way, is a French word meaning pick up all your stuff and carry it for a bit.) Along this mile-long trek south, it is recommended you either wear a head net or be prepared to put on plenty of bug repellent, especially in late spring and early summer.

At the junction with the west-east trail running from Whitefish Lake to the southern shoreline of Clark Lake, hikers can either turn west for a 0.5-mile hike to Whitefish Lake, or head east for 1.5 miles toward the southern shore of Clark Lake. There are no campsites along this southern leg of the trail. Before reaching the end of the leg, hikers have several options for more diversity. One option: about 1 mile from the junction, the portage to the very popular fishing lake called Loon Lake crosses the trail. It is only about 400 yards to this excellent smallmouth bass lake. To camp here, hikers will need to portage a canoe; the campsites are all reached by water.

Another option: nearly 300 yards farther east is a junction with the deepest penetrating trails in the Sylvania tract. Area managers advise hikers not to travel these routes from the west shore campsites, since they are not loops and only the shorter north trail has campsites. To access them, hike on instead for about 50 yards to the junction with the 0.5-mile trail to Badger campsite, and set up camp there. You can plan an outing into the interior of the Sylvania wilderness for the next day.

The southern trail into the wilderness area is approximately 3.5 miles long and will eventually lead along the eastern shores of Deer Island Lake and over the portage to rarely visited Cub Lake. The trail is an easy hike for even the casual hiker, but cuts through fairly low-lying areas, which can mean bugs—lots of them in late spring and early summer. On the southeast corner of Deer

Island Lake hikers will pass a junction with a cross-country ski trail. Keep to the right to finish the trek to Cub Lake.

The northern trail branches off the southern trail after the first mile from the junction with the Clark Lake trail, but swings north near Germain Lake. Since there are campsites available along this leg of the trail, hikers might want to consider a stay along this route at Crooked, Mountain, or East Bear lakes. About 1 mile past the fork in the trail, hikers can take a 0.5-mile side trip to High Lake, but keep in mind that this is not a loop; you will have to retrace your steps.

Once you have explored the interior of the Sylvania, the route around Clark Lake heads back north along the shore of the lake. From this point, an optional 2-mile trail will get you to the park access road, but you will have a 1-mile walk back to the parking lot along a busy paved road. Passing the junction with this "shortcut" back to civilization, the main trail continues along the shore of Clark Lake, reaching the first of three campsites, Pine, about 0.75 mile from the shortcut junction. The next two campsites, Balsam and Ash, are side by side about 0.75 mile beyond.

From the last of the campsites, Ash, it is only about 0.5 mile back to the start point at the launch site.

19   BAY DE NOC–GRAND ISLAND TRAIL

Overview

The Bay de Noc–Grand Island Trail traces the pathway used by American Indians and fur traders moving wares from the shores of Lake Superior and northern Lake Michigan. Chippewa people used the route to portage canoes and supplies. The voyageurs, quick to use convenient routes to reach fur markets, kept the pathway alive. The 40 miles of trail closely shadow several rivers and lakes, including the Whitefish River, making this route one of the longest historic trails in the state.

The linear trail starts on its south end near the Lake Michigan community of Rapid River and terminates near Lake Ackerman, several miles back from the Lake Superior shoreline. To finish the trek between the lakes, hikers can follow the Au Train River to its outlet into Lake Superior.

The terrain is fairly level and stretches through conifer and hardwood stands and the rolling, almost rhythmic, small hills created by retreating glaciers. Wildflowers and wildlife are common sights. Hikers must deal with a fair number of small creek crossings, but those who fish will find more than a few willing brook trout in the several small creeks and brooks. The trail shadows the Whitefish River for nearly half the distance, offering great views of the river valley and the countryside to the west of it. Hikers will encounter a large number of sandy county roads, so a good map is essential for navigating. Footing is generally good, but be prepared to deal with watery crossing points.

19   BAY DE NOC-GRAND ISLAND TRAIL

General description: A historic trail across the narrow waist of the Upper Peninsula, from Lake Michigan's north shore to Lake Superior.

General location: The central Upper Peninsula, passing through Alger and Delta counties.

Maps: USGS Forest Lake, Lake Stella, Poplar Lake, Baker Creek, and Rapid River quads. The Forest Service supplies an information sheet and map of the trail, but it contains only major landmarks, roads, and waterways.

Degree of difficulty: Moderate, because of the distance involved. The terrain is not particularly challenging, but because this is a linear trail, you may have to retrace earlier tracks. Water crossings can be negotiated easily and should not present undue hardship.

Length: 40 miles. There are no spur trails, but numerous sandy county roads crisscross the area and could be used as start points for shorter excursions.

Elevations: Minor. The surrounding area is generally flat with a few gentle hills.

Special attractions: Whitefish River valley views, glacial terrain, wildflowers; wildlife, stream fishing.

Best season: Fall, when forest color is at its prime. In autumn, low areas are minus the squadrons of flying, biting insects. If you visit the area midweek, the trail may be deserted. Hunters use the area after September 15, so dress in bright clothing and stay alert to the possibility, especially near road crossings.

For more information: Munising Ranger District, Hiawatha National Forest, 601 Cedar Street, Munising, MI 49862, (906) 387-2512, or Rapid River Ranger District, Hiawatha National Forest, 8181 U.S. Highway 2, Rapid River, MI 49878, (906) 474-6442.

Finding the trailheads: The southern trailhead near Rapid River can be reached by driving east on U.S. Highway 2 for 2 miles to County Road 509. Turn left onto CR 509 and drive 1.5 miles north to the parking lot and trailhead on the west side of the road. The midpoint trailhead is also on CR 509, but is 15 miles farther north, on the east side of the road. The northern trailhead can be reached by driving southwest of Munising on Michigan Highway 94. The parking lot and trailhead are on the north side of M-94 opposite Ackerman Lake.

The hike: Following the Bay de Noc Trail is easy because of the trail care and grooming provided courtesy of the horse riders who also make good use of the route. The pathway is wide and cleared of low-lying branches to make it easier for the trail riders, which makes it doubly easy for hikers. The route is marked with blue signposts that are easily seen; turns in the trail are marked in yellow.

From the trailhead, the pathway swings almost immediately north and passes through a large stand of jackpine. About 2 miles from the start, hikers make their first of many water crossings over Bills Creek. The trail shadows the Whitefish River to the west for much of the 22 miles to the midpoint trailhead, and keeps CR 509 on its right for nearly the entire 40 miles to Ackerman Lake.

Nearly 2 miles from the first water crossing the habitat changes from conifers to hardwoods and open fields. This is also the point where having a map

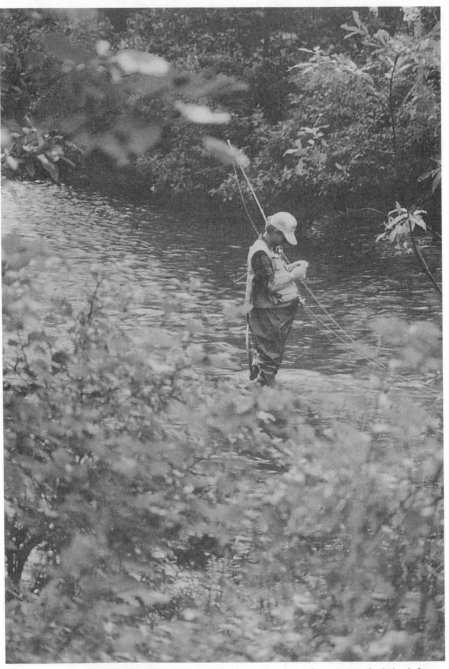
Hikers are advised to pause at the river and stream crossings to try their luck for a trout dinner.

becomes vital, since the trail is crossed by a number of sand roads and fire-breaks as well as areas of large-scale logging. About 5 miles farther north, the trail crosses Haymeadow Creek. Here hikers can end their first day on the trail at the only established campground along the trail, Haymeadow Creek Camp. To reach the campground, turn right on the first two-track past the bridge over the creek to CR 509. Then head south for 0.4 mile to the campground. You will have to retrace your steps to get back to the trail, since there is no loop to make things easier.

About 3 miles from Haymeadow Creek, the trail crosses CR 509 and stays on the east side of the road for about 5 miles as it passes through the upper end of the Whitefish River valley. Lower and Middle Eighteenmile lakes appear east of the trail before the trail crosses CR 509 once more, staying on the other side this time for 3.5 miles.

At a junction with County Road 440, the trail switches back to the east side of CR 509 for the final 0.5 mile to the midpoint trailhead. At this point hikers leave Delta County and enter Alger County. From the midpoint trailhead, the pathway continues for 2.5 miles on the east side of CR 509 (known as H-05 in Alger County) crossing back to the west side of the road between Saul Lake to the east and Davies Lake to the west. The trail stays west of the road for 4 miles before crossing it once again, crossing County Road M-27 a mile later. About 1.5 miles farther, the trail crosses H-05 again and shoulders briefly the west shore of the Cleveland Cliffs Basin before swinging around the west shore of Lake Seventeen.

The final few miles of the trail jog left and right occasionally as the pathway winds its way to the northern trailhead at Ackerman Lake. Hikers have the option of hiking east for 10 miles along M-94 to Munising to reach the shores of Lake Superior, or going 2 miles west across the Au Train River, then north on H-05 along the river, to reach the lake.

20   HIGH COUNTRY PATHWAY

Overview

Veteran hikers have labeled the High Country Pathway "The Hike Assembled By Committee," since the terrain and habitat change abruptly and constantly. The complete loop takes an experienced hiker nearly seven days to complete, provided he or she doesn't make too many stops to fish or take note of the diverse flora and fauna along the trail. Wet and wild, flat and hilly are just a few of the possible combinations to be found along the 70-mile-long pathway—and that's before you include the possible combinations mentioned above. But the varied hike welcomes all ages and all levels of experience, and with a little planning, this trek can be the most enjoyable "wilderness" hike in the state.

The High Country Pathway is accessible from a good number of northern Lower Peninsula communities, depending on the start point you choose. There are also plenty of opportunities to make shorter jaunts into the heart of Pigeon River Country State Forest and the surrounding territory.

The Pigeon River region is home to the largest free-roaming herd of elk found east of the Mississippi River. Some 1,200 elk range here. It is not uncommon to observe white-tailed deer, wild turkeys, or black bears, along with a host of other small animals, along the trail. Eagles and ospreys soar over the region, and more than a hundred other species of birds call this area home. One of the best brook trout streams in the Midwest, the Black River, flows through the area. The Pigeon River and McMasters Creek are also good trout fisheries. Lakes encountered along the trail offer fishing for everything from rainbow trout and pan fish to northern pike and bass.

General description: A 70-mile loop through some of the most diverse environments in Michigan.

General location: The northeastern corner is 8 miles south of Onaway (Presque Isle County) on Michigan Highway 33; the southeastern corner is 5 miles north of Atlanta (Montmorency County) on M-33; and the western entry points are nearly 12 miles east of Vanderbilt (Otsego County), or 9 miles east of Wolverine (Cheboygan County).

Maps: It takes nine USGS quads to cover the High Country trail system: Onaway, Tower, Afton, Lake Geneva, Silver Lake, Hardwood Lake, Atlanta, Hetherton, and Saunders Creek. A more-convenient but less-detailed pocket sized trail description is available from the Pigeon River Country Association, P.O. Box 122, Gaylord, MI 49735.

Degree of difficulty: Easy to moderate. The entire hike can be handled by hikers of all levels of experience, but planning is a must, especially during the wet and insect seasons.

Length: 70 miles. The loop can be broken easily into shorter segments, using the ten campgrounds scattered around its perimeter as start points. Loops off the main trail range from the 2.5 mile Sinkhole Pathway in the northeast to the 11-mile Shingle Mill Pathway in the southwest.

Elevations: Rolling terrain, with no difficult ascents or descents; there are several climbs of 100 feet or less at the northwest corner of the trail.

Special attractions: Wildlife, fishing.

Best season: Late summer, because of fewer flying insects to interfere with a hiker's enjoyment. Fall colors paint a beautiful panorama, but the area attracts hunters from mid-September until snow blocks access to smaller roads in the area.

For more information: Department of Natural Resources, Region II Headquarters, Roscommon, MI 48653, (517) 275-5151; Pigeon River Country State Forest Headquarters, (517) 983-4101; Pigeon River Country Association, P.O. Box 122, Gaylord, MI 49735.

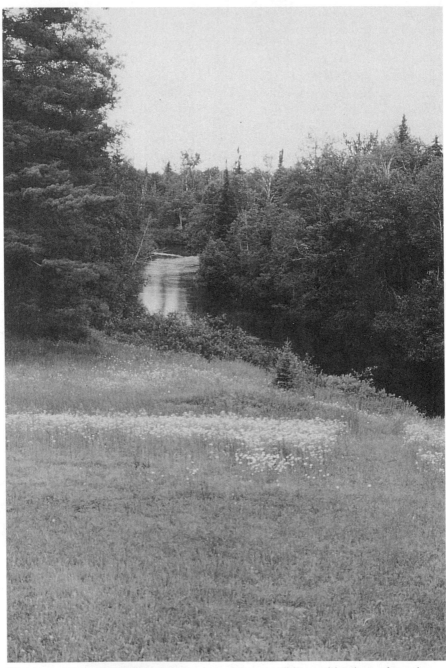

Wet and wild, flat and hilly are just a few of the possible combinations of terrain found along the 70-mile long pathway.

Finding the trailheads: With ten state forest campgrounds and a state park, plus nearly three dozen road crossings to serve as start points for a hike along the High Country Pathway, the list of possible trailheads and directions to find them would fill pages. The most practical starting points are the ten campgrounds below, which not only provide easy and unmistakable access to the Pathway, but are strung along the 70-mile loop like so many pearls in a necklace:

1. Pigeon Bridge State Forest Campground—Take Sturgeon Valley Road east out of Vanderbilt for about 12 miles to reach the campground.

2. Elk Hill State Forest Campground—Head east out of Vanderbilt on Sturgeon Valley Road for 15 miles to reach this start point.

3. Pigeon River State Forest Campground—Near the junction with Hardwood Lake Road and Sturgeon Valley Road, nearly 14 miles east of Vanderbilt.

4. Pine Grove State Forest Campground—Head east out of Wolverine on Webb Road for about 9 miles and turn south for about 3 miles on Campsite Road. This trailhead is also used as a starting point for the Shingle Mill Pathway (see reference in hike description).

5. Round Lake State Forest Campground—Head east from Vanderbilt on Sturgeon Valley Road for about 13 miles, then south about 2 miles on Round Lake Road. The Pathway is connected to the campground by a 0.5-mile trail to the north.

6. Town Corner State Forest Campground—Head north from Atlanta on Michigan Highway 33 for 5 miles. Turn west on Rouse Road for 11 miles before turning north onto County Road 495, leading to the campground. The Pathway is connected to the campground by an easy 0.5-mile trail to the west.

7. Jackson Lake State Forest Campground—Drive north of Atlanta on M-33 for 7 miles, then east on County Road 624 for 0.5 mile. The Pathway is reached via a 1.5-mile trail that is also part of the Clear Lake-Jackson Lake Pathway.

8. Clear Lake State Park—The park is 9 miles north of Atlanta on M-33. The Pathway is reached via a 0.75-mile trail east of the park across M-33.

9. Tomahawk Lake State Forest Campground—Reached by driving 3 miles east on Tomahawk Lake Highway, off M-33. The Pathway passes along the eastern edge of the campground.

10. Shoepac Lake State Forest Campground—Head south from Onaway on M-33 for 8 miles, then turn east on County Road 634 for the 3-mile drive to the campground. A 0.25-mile trail connects the campground to the Pathway and the nearby Sinkhole Pathway.

The hike: The High Country Pathway has as many start points as it does access points, but the trail from Clear Lake State Park, on the eastern edge of the system, described here, is one of the best.

Hikers will use the first leg of the Clear Lake Nature Trail to reach the start point, about 1 mile from the trailhead. The two trails merge at a gravel pit located a few hundred yards east of M-33. From here, the pathway swings north toward its first major natural landmark, Tomahawk Creek Flooding, some 9 miles away. The first section of trail passes through gentle terrain that

CLEAR LAKE NATURE TRAIL

was once the hub of activity for the region's logging industry at the turn of the century. The area is the site of the north's last great forest fire, which occurred in 1939. The trail is sandy in places, making walking a bit tough, so take your time. Low sand hills studded with stands of jackpine dominate the landscape along this section.

One of the Midwest's finest brook trout streams, the Black River, flows through the area.

As you approach the Tomahawk Creek Flooding, don't be afraid to vary your path and do a little exploring. A small, primitive campground at the northeast corner of the flooding is a nice spot to set up camp, especially if you are looking for quiet. Water is available here, and so is some of the most productive fishing along the entire shoreline—this can provide a tasty respite from trail fare for the patient angler. The structure along the shoreline hides cooperative bluegill, crappie, and other pan fish and even the occasional largemouth bass or cruising northern pike.

From the campground, 2 miles of easy hiking bring hikers to Tomahawk Lake State Forest Campground. Farther north, in 0.75 mile, is Shoepac Lake State Forest Campground. These two campgrounds are both well developed and have all the simple pleasures—the things road-campers demand and trail hikers find a real treat. Both campgrounds, though out-of-the-way, are popular destinations during summer and early fall. Deer hunters use these campgrounds as main camps as late as November.

North of Shoepac Lake is the trailhead for the 2.5-mile Sinkhole Pathway Loop. This 2,600-acre area has been closed to all motorized travel, providing a serene setting still changing beneath the surface; the underlying karst is constantly being dissolved and the surface layer sinks to conform to these changes in the limestone bedrock. The loop trail actually is divided into two loops—a 0.75-mile loop around the first two major sinkholes, and a 1.5-mile trail that not only includes the other three major sinkholes in the region, but features a wooden stairway to the bottom of one of the deepest "sinks" in Presque Isle County. The floor of this sinkhole is more than 100 feet lower than the sur-

SINKHOLE PATHWAY

face of nearby Shoepac Lake. The loops are easy to follow and well marked. Improvements made to the area include rustic fencing put up to protect the fragile slopes of the sinkholes; along the northern sections of the trails, wood chips have been used to retard plant growth that might try to reclaim the path.

The Sinkhole Pathway rejoins the High Country Pathway. The next 27 miles, from Shoepac Lake to Pine Grove State Forest Campground, is the longest stretch without a prepared or formal campground and, more importantly, without good drinking water. Hikers should carry all necessary water or have the gear needed to purify water from streams and lakes along the trail. They should also be prepared for primitive camping.

From the Sinkhole Pathway, the main trail takes a decided westward bent along the fringe of a popular lake-pocked area that can be quite "moist" in the spring and after heavy rainfalls. The trail usually poses no problem for even the casual hiker, but its condition can change dramatically with added moisture.

Once across M-33, the trail crosses a good number of small streams, including Canada Creek, which merits prospecting for native brook trout. Hikers will cross into Cheboygan County 1 mile after crossing Canada Creek. The terrain rises and falls rather significantly along this 2-mile stretch of the trail, with hills rising several hundred feet then falling into marshy pockets.

The next major water obstacle, the trout-rich Black River, is preceded by another significant rise. These high areas provide an excellent spot to set up camp, since they get up out of the bug-infested lowlands. Plus, the nearby Black River serves up some of the very best brook trout fishing found anywhere in the Midwest. The water appears to be crystal-clear, but treat it before drinking or cooking with it.

About 2 miles farther west the trail drops back into the marshy wetlands surrounding Duby Lake. The swamps around the lake are alive with wildlife and, in the spring, squadrons of needle-nosed mosquitos and black flies. The lake is a picturesque 400-yard hike off the pathway, but avoid it during bug season unless you intend your visit to be a brief one. A short 400 yards farther west on the trail, hikers will find the marker pointing the way to McLavery Lake. This beautiful, remote lake is framed by white birch and delivers a view well worth the 0.5-mile hike to reach it.

Back on the main trail, the next 3.5 miles go through some of the finest mosquito habitat found anywhere in Michigan. Be prepared to use plenty of bug dope. The trail through this stretch is rated easy, but it can be damp during early spring.

Dog Lake Flooding is the next landmark to the south, about 250 yards from the trail. The lake contains a few fish, but even local fishermen stay away and won't attempt crossing its boggy shoreline until winter has solidified things. The flooding attracts large numbers of waterfowl and other wildlife, including osprey and an occasional bald eagle.

The High Country Pathway turns to the south 1.5 miles from Dog Lake Flooding and takes on a new face as well as a new direction. The wetlands and swamps are replaced by hardwood stands and dry ridgelines. The "downhill" run in a 7-mile hike through a mix of upland habitats eventually leads to the banks of the Pigeon River. At the end of this segment of the Pathway, hikers will find the remote Pine Grove State Forest Campground. This site may not be as cozy as the local Holiday Inn, but it is a welcome break from rustic camping along the more isolated northern shoulders of the trail. Toilets and drinking water are available, along with prepared tent sites that make setting up camp easier. The campground is on the east bank of the Pigeon River, a favorite hot spot for local trout fishermen throughout spring and early summer. This site is back from the normal flow of traffic, so midweek hikers will find that they have the area pretty much to themselves.

Heading south from Pine Grove, the trail weaves through stands of large maples, beeches, and even oaks. About 4 miles from Pine Grove, it merges with the first loop of the Shingle Mill Pathway. Here, the trail swings east for 2 miles until the combined trails reach the banks of the Pigeon River once again. The combined pathways shadow the river for 1.5 miles before entering the Pigeon River State Forest Campground. A second campground, the Pigeon Bridge State Forest Campground, is just 2 miles farther south, should the first campground be too crowded.

A must–stop for all hikers on the High Country Pathway is the Pigeon River Country State Forest Headquarters, located 1 mile south of the Pigeon

SHINGLE MILL PATHWAY

River campground. The remaining buildings in the complex were built by the Civilian Conservation Corps in the early 1930s, from logs cut in the surrounding forest. Locally cut red and white pine logs were used to construct all of the buildings in use today, including the staff house, which served as the first conservation school in Michigan.

Hikers who want to explore the loops of the Shingle Mill Pathway should be prepared to stay a few days since there are 18 miles of path to check out. Loops in the pathway range from 0.75 to 11 miles long. The five loops accommodate hikers of all experience levels, even though the distance of the outer loops has given rise to a moderate classification for the trails.

The High Country Pathway traces the eastern edge of the Shingle Mill Pathway for 6.5 miles until the combined trails end at the Pigeon River State Forest Campground. The two shortest loops—0.75 miles and 1.25 miles—make easy day hikes; they parallel the eastern bank of the Pigeon River for half their lengths before dropping back to the campground. A 6-mile loop follows the course of the Pigeon River for 2 miles before turning east on a cross-country trek to join the High Country Pathway at the headquarters complex mentioned earlier. From here it continues north for 1 mile to a point just north of the Pigeon River campground. Cross over the Pigeon River using the road bridge. The trail swings nearly due west for 1.5 miles before turning back south, meandering off and on the western banks of the Pigeon River.

A 10-mile loop follows the same trace as the 6-mile loop, but continues north from the point where the shorter loop swings west. The trail shares the same route as the High Country Pathway for nearly 1.5 miles before turning west for 1 mile to reach a campsite at the southern end of Grass Lake. From the campsite, the trail heads north for 0.5 mile before turning south for the 3-mile hike back to the start point. This loop joins the southbound leg of the 6-mile loop just south of Ford Lake.

The longest loop, the 11-mile trail, picks up where the 10-mile trail turns west, continuing north for slightly more than 0.5 mile to reach the Cornwall campsite. The trail mirrors the High Country Pathway for 2 miles before turning south to blend with the southbound leg of the 10- and 6-mile Shingle Mill loops.

Hikers rejoining the High Country Pathway pick up the trail from the Pigeon Bridge State Forest Campground. Here the trail begins its eastern swing across the bottom of the trail system, cutting through rolling terrain dominated at first by impressive red pines and later by a mix of jack pine, aspen, and other second-growth stands of timber. The first trail marker is for a spur trail leading south to Round Lake State Forest Campground. The signpost is only 0.5 mile from the campground you just left. The short, easy hike to this campground puts the hiker into a setting of tall red pines and a lake filled with rainbow trout courtesy of the Department of Natural Resources. Cold, clear drinking water is available at the site.

The next 9 miles of trail are a walk back through the history of commercial logging in the region. Trail users pass through hundreds of acres of second-growth forest fostered by the industry that took millions of board feet of lumber to metropolitan markets. Be sure to keep a lookout for the remains of the Black River Overlook Tower, just west of Walled Lake. The tower was just one of many scattered throughout the region; fire watch stations have now been replaced by aircraft flying patrols over the area.

JACKSON LAKE HIKING TRAIL

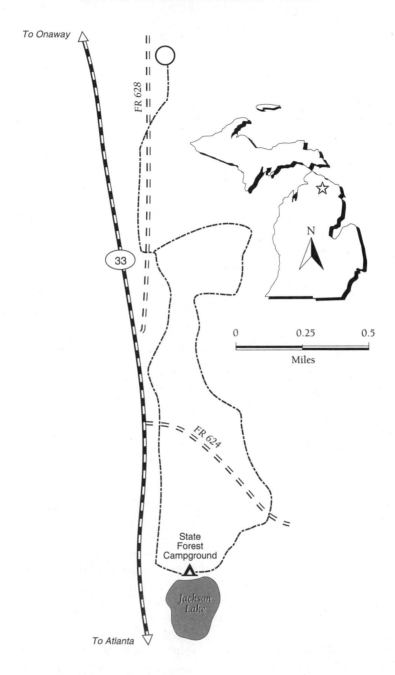

In just 1 mile farther you will find the marker for Town Corner State Forest Campground. The campground is an easy 0.5-mile hike east off the Pathway, offering good water, toilets, and a chance to swim in the warm waters of Town Corner Lake. Fishermen will find the resident largemouth bass population a challenge.

Elk sightings are fairly common over the next 10 miles. Loggers leveled the region under the "whole trees" concept, hauling away logs and truckloads of chips, leaving the entire area open to natural reforestation. The attraction for the elk is obvious: the young aspen provide a standing smorgasbord of the elk's favorite food. Deer and upland birds are also fairly common in this area.

The trail blends with the southwest corner of the Clear Lake Nature Trail for the final 2 miles back to the state park and the trailhead. The Clear Lake Nature Trail is a 5-mile loop around Clear Lake, the eastern and southern lengths of which are shared with the traces of the High Country Pathway. The trailhead, mentioned earlier in the hike description, is located in the parking lot between the two Clear Lake campgrounds in the state park. The sections of the trail that are shared by the Pathway are more than 1 mile from the nearest services in the park. So make certain you take along plenty of water and a day pack with necessary items, such as a first-aid kit.

At the southeast corner of the Clear Lake Nature Trail, about 2 miles from the trailhead, is the junction with the Jackson Lake Hiking Trail. The trail continues to the west from this point for 1 mile before swinging back to the north at the Clear Lake Day Use Area. Water and toilets are available here. The Jackson Lake Hiking Trail heads due south from its junction with the Clear Lake trail, along the west side of M-33 for about 3 miles to the Jackson Lake State Forest Campground. The return loop back to the junction with the Clear Lake trail is a meandering 4.5 miles through hilly and wooded terrain dominated by a mix of large hardwoods and pines.

21   SHORE-TO-SHORE TRAIL

Overview

The Shore-To-Shore Trail was the idea of trail riders looking for a lengthy horseback trek from shore to shore across the northern tip of Michigan's Lower Peninsula. With the help of Michigan Senator William Milliken, the trail was established in 1962. The 220-mile trail connects the town of Empire, on Lake Michigan, with the Lake Huron community of Oscoda. Hikers need to be aware of the use of the trail by horseback riders, but the trail is open for all users but bicyclists. It is the longest continuous trail in the Lower Peninsula.

The trail offers a look into rural Michigan, and although it doesn't trace a path through the wilds like the North Country Trail does, it follows many northern back roads and river valleys. The Shore-To-Shore Trail is easy to hike as it follows roads and well-marked pathways through stands of conifers and hardwoods, making its way across the northern tip of the state. A group of horseback trail riders called The Michigan Trail Riders provides a complete set of maps, as well as a trail guide, to help hikers cross the state by this route.

Although the trail is fairly "urban," it avoids the tourist destinations of Michigan's north country. Its scenery—some of the most beautiful the state offers—ranks highest on the list of special attractions. Another attraction is the Kirtland warbler habitat near Grayling and the banks of the Au Sable River, through which hikers pass. The rare Kirtland warbler is carefully watched over by the Department of Natural Resources; it is a treat to see and hear. Mixed upland and lowland habitats mean that hikers will see a wide variety of birds, animals, and other creatures as they hike from shore to shore.

General description: A horse and hiker trail across the Lower Peninsula.
General location: West-east across the northern Lower Peninsula, running from Empire, on Lake Michigan, to Oscoda, on U.S. Highway 23 and Lake Huron.
Maps: USGS Empire, Burdickville, Platte River, Lake Ann, Grawn, Mayfield, Jacks Landing, South Boardman, Kalkaska, Leetsville, Westwood, Starvation Lake, Frederic, Lake Margrethe, Grayling, Wakeley Lake, Roscommon North, Eldorado, Luzerne, Island Lake, Mack Lake, McKinley, Goodar, Alcona Dam Pond, Hale, Loud Dam, Sid Town, Foote Site Village, and Oscoda quads. The Michigan Trail Riders' brochure and guidebook, with accompanying maps, are valuable in sorting out the trail on the quads.

The trail provides a chance to hike through some of the most beautiful scenery Michigan has to offer, especially in the fall.

Degree of difficulty: Moderate, more because of length than the condition of the pathway. Since the trail traces roads and two-track jeep paths, much of the base provides great footing. Still, there are sandy stretches, eroded to the point of being tough walking. Plan to break this hike into manageable segments, according to your timetable and hiking ability.

Length: 220 miles, with two additional spurs leading north (86 miles) and south (44 miles).

Elevations: The trail crosses varied terrain, but is generally hilly. It is easily managed if hikers aren't in a rush to reach the opposite shore.

Special attractions: Cross-state route, wildlife, rare Kirtland warblers.

Best season: Fall, when river valleys, especially the Au Sable, come alive with autumn color.

For more information: Michigan Trail Riders Association, 1650 Ormond Road, White Lake, MI 48383-2344, (810) 889-3624; Traverse City Chamber of Commerce, Traverse City, MI 449684, (616) 947-5075; Michigan Department of Natural Resources Forest, Management Division, P.O. Box 30452, Lansing, MI 48909, (517) 373-1275.

Finding the trailheads: Hikers can approach the trail from either end. The two main trailheads are in the communities of Empire and Oscoda. The Empire trailhead (used for this hike description) is at the junction of Michigan Highways 22 and 72. The trail follows M-72 east for several miles out of town. The Oscoda trailhead starts at the junction of River Road and U.S. Highway 23. Many hikers prefer to walk the short additional distance from the shores of Lakes Michigan and Huron to fully appreciate the shore-to-shore nature of this pathway.

The hike: Going east from the Lake Michigan shoreline to the Lake Huron coast, on the sunrise side, the Shore-To-Shore Trail makes use of rural roadways, two-track jeep paths, and a variety of cross-country trails that follow river valleys. Hikers on this lengthy trail may be disappointed at first to have to spend so much time along the shoulders of prepared roads, but the scenery and relative ease of the hike will erase many of those sentiments.

From the Empire trailhead, the first day on the Shore-to-Shore is a relatively easy one, an 8-mile jaunt east from Empire to Garey Lake Camp. The route follows M-72 east for 3.5 miles to an intersection with Kitlinger Road. The trail turns south on Kitlinger Rd., and follows it for 1.5 miles before turning east for another 1 mile. The trail then leaves the roadway, continuing eastward for another 2.5 miles toward the first night camping area at Garey Lake Camp. If the lower campground is filled, try the overflow area on the hill to the west.

Views of the surrounding countryside are worth a pause or two as you leave Garey Lake Camp. The trail heads nearly due south, crossing Pettingill Road and entering Benzie County. The path heads cross-country for the next 5.5 miles. The route then follows several small two-track roads until it reaches Oakley Road, following it east for 3.5 miles.

The trail traces Mill Road south for 1 mile before turning east again, this time onto Bronson Lake Road for the next 2.5-mile segment. It's only about 2.5

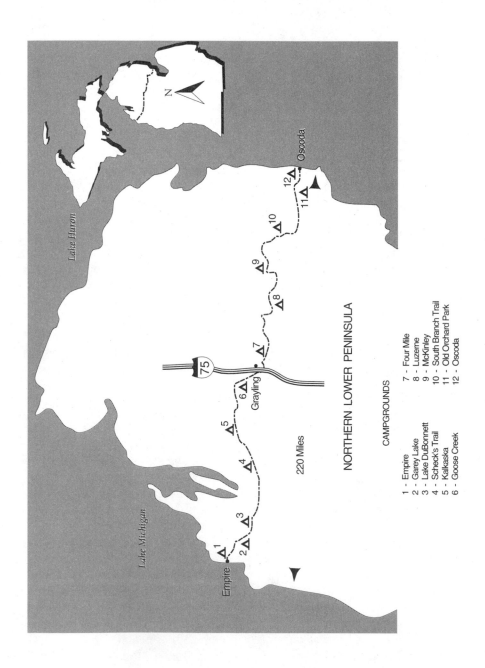

NORTHERN LOWER PENINSULA

220 Miles

CAMPGROUNDS

1 - Empire
2 - Garey Lake
3 - Lake DuBonnett
4 - Scheck's Trail
5 - Kalkaska
6 - Goose Creek

7 - Four Mile
8 - Luzerne
9 - McKinley
10 - South Branch Trail
11 - Old Orchard Park
12 - Oscoda

miles to the next campground, but the trail meanders north on Lake Ann Road for 0.5 mile to a small two-track on the right (east) where the trail swings east for the final 2 miles of the day. Hikers will turn onto another two-track and cross into Grand Traverse County before they reach Lake DuBonnett Camp, the second night's destination. Lake DuBonnett is also known as Mud Lake to the locals. The camp offers water and toilets, and is a nice spot to break for the night.

From Lake DuBonnett, the trail follows a gravel road east for 2.4 miles to its intersection with Long Road. The trail crosses the road and heads nearly due south on another gravel road for 1.5 miles before swinging easterly for 0.5 mile; here it joins U.S. Highway 31. Hikers must follow US 31 east for 0.25 mile to Grawn Road, then follow this road for 2.5 miles to Vance Road for the next 2.5-mile leg, still heading nearly due east across Grand Traverse County.

Hikers next enter the Boardman River valley, stepping off the shoulders of paved roads and onto gravel for the next 3.8 miles. At the end of this stretch of shared pathway, the trail takes a decided cross-country tack as it heads east down the river valley for the next 2.5 miles. The cross-country jaunt ends at a gravel road leading into the community of Mayfield.

The trail follows County Road 611 north for 0.5 mile before it swings east again onto Mayfield Road for about 2 miles. At this point, the trail swings northeast, heading for Scheck's Trail Camp on the banks of the Boardman River. The camp offers not only prepared sites, but all the comforts of a modern campground. It's a good place for a third night's stop.

From Scheck's Trail Camp, the trail crosses the Boardman River, heading northeasterly, and Boardman Road. It continues on gravel roads and sections of pathway for the next 3 miles. The trail next crosses Supply Road, continues northeast for 2.3 miles, then crosses Broomhead Road.

For the next 3 miles, hikers shadow North River Road but leave the road-way just after crossing into Kalkaska County. The next 5.5 miles of trail follow a series of tracks and gravel county roads as hikers head for the next campground at Kalkaska Camp, also known as Rapid River Camp. Hikers will have to cross M-72 heading north. After reaching Old Michigan Highway 72, they will follow that road southeast; it leads to the camp entrance. Kalkaska Camp offers all the comforts of a large campground. Please respect the private property along the entrance road.

Leaving the campground, hikers will head cross-country to the northeast, crossing the old Penn Central tracks east of Kalkaska. Once across the tracks, hikers will enter Mayhem Swamp, also known as Kalkaska Swamp, prompting many to remember why they decided to wait until late in the bug season to attempt this hike. At the junction of Hagni Road and Darrach Road, hikers will turn south for the 1-mile hike to the next junction with Myers Road.

The trail heads east from this point for 2 miles, drops south for 1 mile, then heads east first on Grass Lake Road and then takes off in an easterly trend cross-country between Grass Lake and Bear Lake. The cross-country trek continues for the next 4.5 miles, crossing Blue Lake Road and continuing east for another 1.5 miles before picking up a gravel road south of the Goose Creek

Flooding. As the trail reaches Goose Creek Road, hikers will step out of Kalkaska County and into Crawford County.

Less than 0.5 mile northeast is the next campground, Goose Creek Camp. The forested area and open spaces hikers pass through before reaching the campground are remnants of an old logging camp. The campsite is on the banks of the Manistee River.

From Goose Creek Camp, the trail takes a southeast heading to pass between Lake Margrethe and the town of Grayling before bending back toward the east. The path heads south for 3 miles and crosses Batterson Road, sharing a short 1-mile stretch of State Forest Road. It then curves south and again goes cross-country for a 3-mile hike to the next series of gravel roads; this section leads to M-72, which hikers must cross.

From the highway crossing, the trail continues south for another 5.5 miles to Four Mile Road. Hikers have the graded shoulders of Four Mile Rd. as a pathway for the next 9 miles as the trace heads due east. About 4.8 miles after stepping onto Four Mile Rd., tired hikers find Four Mile Camp, which appears on the right. This large campsite has all of the needs for a pleasant night's stay.

From the campground, the trail continues east for another 5 miles along Four Mile Rd. (which hikers by now feel is misnamed) to the intersection with Chase Bridge Road. Crossing this latter road, the trail continues east along a series of narrow, sandy roads. It goes 4.5 miles in this way, until it intersects with M-72 once more. The trail crosses to the north side of the highway and shadows the roadway for the next 4 miles before crossing back to the south side. The terrain here is a bit hilly and the trail is sandy because of the use by horses, but with a little patience it can be easily negotiated. Keep an eye out for rare Kirtland warblers through this area.

About 1 mile south of M-72, the pathway again takes an eastern heading as it trails toward the next campsite, at Luzerne Camp, 6.5 miles from this turn. The trail passes over a series of rolling hills covered by mixed pines and hardwoods. Two miles after making the eastern swing, hikers enter Oscoda County.

From Luzerne Camp, the pathway meanders east, following a series of two-track roads and forest roads to cross M-33 about 5 miles south of the city of Mio. The trail shadows the right shoulder of the highway for about 1 mile before resuming its northeast meander toward Lake Huron.

Nearly 7 miles farther on, hikers will cross Forest Road 4146, staying on the north side of the road for about 2 miles before crossing back to the south to continue the eastward trek. Midway along that 2-mile stretch of the trail, the next campsite, McKinley Camp, appears on the left, along the southern banks of the Au Sable River.

The remainder of the hike is along the Au Sable River and its wide, forested valley. After crossing FR 4146, the trail shadows the Au Sable River for 8 miles as it makes its way south toward Alcona Pond. Hikers cross into Alcona County about 2.5 miles before reaching the pond. The trail traces the western and southern shores of the impoundment for nearly 3 miles before swinging southeast for the 3.5 miles to the Iosco County line.

The next campground, South Branch Trail Camp, is just 1.25 miles farther along the trail. From the campground, the trail continues southeast for 4 miles until it crosses Rollaway Road, crossing Michigan Highway 65 in 0.25 mile. The path directs itself more easterly once across the highway, shadowing M-65 for about 5 miles before staying on the high ridges above River Road, a National Scenic Byway segment that runs east all the way into Oscoda. After crossing Forest Road 4421, the roadway to your left is River Road. The trail and the roadway both lead to the same place so, if the trail has become too much, the shoulder of the road will deliver you to the same destination.

About 7.5 miles farther east, the trail crosses River Rd., continuing on the northern side along the bank of the Au Sable River. The trail stays on this side of the roadway for the next 6 miles before it crosses back to the southern side of the roadway. The final campsite along the Shore-To-Shore Trail is located 0.1 mile past that crossover, but you must recross River Rd. to enter Old Orchard Park Camp.

The final 11 miles to Oscoda will seem tame after hiking the previous 200-plus; the trail levels out with few hills left to conquer before reaching the shores of Lake Huron. As you sit on the sand of the lakeshore and think over your cross-state trek, it won't take much to figure out just why the fur traders used water routes.

22   WATERLOO-PINCKNEY RECREATION HIKING TRAIL

Overview

The Waterloo-Pinckney Trail links two of southern Michigan's most popular recreation spots: the Waterloo and Pinckney recreation areas, which are easily accessible to all major metropolitan areas of southeastern Michigan and thus available to the largest segment of the state's population. The Waterloo-Pinckney trail system is 1 hour driving time west of Detroit and is within 2 hours of all major urban areas in the heavily populated southern half of the state.

Although the location in urban southern Michigan may seem unappealing to some hikers, the trail carefully avoids any exposure to that environment. The Waterloo-Pinckney Recreation Trail mixes habitats and scenic vistas that rival many other areas of the state. Although not as rugged as trails in the western Upper Peninsula or as remote as Isle Royale, this trail system has unique upland, lowland and water habitats and is unconnected to the urban sprawl just an hour in any direction. The area holds more than a dozen lakes and a greater number of small streams and creeks within its boundaries, along with upland forests, high ridges, and lowland marshes and bogs, all laced together by a trail system that is both challenging and hikeable. The trail provides access to perhaps the greatest mix of bird habitats in the region, offering birding opportunities that cannot be found anywhere else in such concentrations.

Camping is available along the trail system at designated campsites only. Access points and campgrounds allow hikers to plan a tailor-made trip through the system, but this is not a hike that should be taken lightly despite the easy nature of the pathway. The trails are well marked, but use by other non-motorized users such as trail riders on horseback and mountain bikers can cause some problems . . . nothing like a traffic jam along the trail! Study maps of the system, plan to use the available campsites to break up the hike into easy segments, and come prepared to enjoy the finest trail system in southern Michigan.

General description: A trail linking two popular recreation sites in the more urban, southern part of Michigan.

General location: Southeastern Michigan, 15 miles west of Ann Arbor and 6 miles east of Jackson. The trail system is less than 60 miles west of the Detroit metroplex.

Maps: Department of Natural Resources trail map (excellent) entitled "Waterloo-Pinckney Trail." Others maps include USGS Chelsea, Grass Lake, Gregory, and Pinckney quads.

Degree of difficulty: Moderate. The several climbs along the more than 36 miles of this trail system are not especially challenging. Hikers should not overextend themselves, however.

Length: 36 miles, from the Portage Lake Day-Use Area at the western end of the trail to the Silver Lake Day-Use Area at the eastern end.

Elevations: A moderate number of steep climbs and equally strenuous descents off ridges will test even the best conditioned hiker, but for the most part the hike can be handled in good form if the trek doesn't turn into a foot race. Several hills rise along the trail, the highest of which is Sackrider Hill at 1,128 feet.

Special attractions: "Backyard" wilderness, birding.

Best seasons: Spring and fall. Once school is out and summer heats up, the area becomes a favorite destination for urban residents looking for "wilderness" close to home. Insects can be a problem, but fall colors can be amazing.

For more information: Waterloo State Recreation Area Headquarters, 16345 McClure Road, Chelsea, MI 48169; Pinckney State Recreation Area Headquarters, 8555 Silverhill, Pinckney, MI 48169.

Finding the trailheads: The major east-west route through the region, Interstate Highway 94, provides the easiest general access from all of southern Michigan, while Interstate Highway 75-U.S. Highway 23 is the main access route from the north.

The eastern trailhead, at park headquarters for the Pinckney Recreation Area, is located at the Silver Lake Day-Use Area. From Michigan Highway 52 near Pinckney, head east on North Territorial Road for five miles to Dexter-Townhall Road and turn left (north). The park entrance will be on the left, about 0.5 mile from the turn. The western trailhead, at the Portage Lake Day-Use Area, is reached from I-94, exiting north on Race Road. Drive north on Race Rd. for about 1 mile to Seymour Road and turn right. The entrance to the day-use area is approximately 0.5 mile on the left.

Other road crossings allow access to the trail, but none with the parking or facilities offered by the two established trailheads.

The hike: This moderate-rated hike can be covered in three days, but doing so will require double-digit mileage days on the trail. The 36-mile hike starts in the Portage Lake Day-Use Area (western trailhead), near the boat ramps. The trail begins as a level, easy walk along a high point overlooking the southern shores of the lake. The view does not last long, since the trail soon heads south to the first of many road crossings. The trail crosses Seymour Road just about 1 mile from the trailhead, and nearly parallels the road for the next 2 miles.

In the next section of trail, you will cross List and then Willis roads before reaching Portage Pond. A short footbridge provides access over the dam at the neck of the impoundment; from there, the trail swings decidedly south again.

Nearly 1 mile past the pond, you will cross Glenn Road and start the first of the major climbs along the route. The trail winds along a ridge before dropping quickly, but hikers will start climbing immediately to the highest point along the trail, Sackrider Hill, at 1,128 feet. From here, the trail drops down to level again as hikers shadow Mount Hope Road to its junction with Katz Road, following Katz Rd. until the trail crosses Glenn Rd. again.

For the next 5 miles the trail swings north and angles a bit toward the next roadway, Baldwin Road. Bird lovers need to keep cameras and binoculars ready because a large flooded area in 0.5 mile hosts large numbers of songbirds and waterfowl, providing plenty of viewing opportunities.

Clear Lake Road is the next landmark. In 0.5 mile farther, another tough climb awaits. This ascent to Pond Lily Lookout is well worth the effort, providing a nice view of the surrounding countryside. An important landmark appears next, after a quick descent from the lookout: Loveland Road, which is the junction of trails that lead to nearby campgrounds. Sugarloaf Lake Campground is the nearest, 1 mile north of the junction.

The trail continues, crossing McClure Road as it heads eastward. Hikers will cross the road several more times as the trail moves past Crooked Lake and interestingly mixed terrain. The trail now turns southeast, passing along the western shore of Mill Lake, then abruptly swinging north to trace the eastern shore, passing an interpretive center and, later, the Mill Lake Outdoor Center. Just past the outdoor center, hikers will cross Bush Road and start the climb to Waterloo Road. A brief hike brings a totally unexpected sight: "Prison Zone" signs indicate that the Cassidy Lake Correctional Facility is nearby. Obey the signs as you move through this area.

The terrain here is quite hilly, but none of these stretches require strenuous climbs. The trail starts to settle into an easterly direction, crossing Cassidy Lake Road before arriving near the entrance to the Green Lake Campground. From the campground, the trail crosses Michigan Highway 52, leaves the Waterloo Recreation Area, and enters Park Lyndon, a Washtenaw County park, for a brief period. This stretch of the trail can be a bit confusing, so keep a sharp eye out for Department of Natural Resources' trail triangles to stay on the main pathway.

Hikers will soon cross North Territorial Road, continue north for 0.5 mile, then swing northeasterly once again. Hikers cross the boundary of the Pinckney Recreation Area at a footbridge over a small creek several hundred yards after the noticeable change in direction. The trail continues to the northeast, crossing Emburn and then Joslip Lake roads, detouring around a large hill and then a marshy area before crossing Hadley Road. From this point, day-use areas and private cottage communities around several of the larger lakes remind hikers of the region's urban nature. The trail from here is fairly hilly in several spots, but even the most tired of hikers can make quick work of the final few miles to the eastern trailhead at the Silver Lake Day-Use Area.

Overview

The Cedar River Pathway is made up of four loops ranging from 2 to 7 miles. These are easy hikes for explorers of all ages. The backdrop of the Cedar River, the remoteness of the western Upper Peninsula, and the mix of rolling hills and upland and riverine environments make this trail system one of the better loop systems in the state.

The pathway is made up of four loops—2 miles, 3.5 miles, 5 miles, and 7 miles long—which offer hikers the opportunity to explore. The trails are wide, well-marked, and easy to follow through a mix of upland and lowland habitats that provide plenty of diversions. Trails follow many of the ridgelines that crisscross the area, as well as "glacier tracks" or eskers left behind retreating sheets of ice.

The western edges of the trail system trace a portion of the Cedar River, the area's greatest attraction. From the fifteen-site rustic campground on the banks of the Cedar River to fishing opportunities, wildlife, and wildflowers, the area is a step into the nature of the region.

The easy-to-follow trails usually provide a smooth adventure into typical Upper Peninsula river habitat, although the total distance of the trail loops can make this a moderate hike for inexperienced hikers. Pace yourself. There are several opportunities to cut the 7-mile hike short if bad weather or other misfortunes arise. The rustic campground located at the southern end of the trails provides a great spot to end the day.

General description: Loops along the wild Cedar River country, for hikers of all ages.

General location: Menominee County, in the Upper Peninsula.

Maps: The Department of Natural Resources office in Gladstone distributes a more-than-adequate trail map.

Degree of difficulty: Easy and well-marked.

Length: 7 miles, but can be broken down into four loops ranging in size from 2 miles to the full 7 miles.

Elevations: Generally hilly terrain, but no difficult climbs.

Special attractions: Glacial geology, and the wild Cedar River.

Best season: Nearby water means that insects will be a problem early in the spring and summer. Late summer and fall are better times to hike the Cedar River pathway, but after mid-September, hunters may be in the area.

For more information: Robert Ziel, Escanaba River State Forest, 6833 U.S. Highway 41/2, Gladstone, MI 49837, (906) 786-2351; Forest Fire Officer, Department of Natural Resources, Stephenson, MI 49987, (906) 753-6317.

Finding the trailheads: The Cedar River Pathway is accessible from U.S. Highway 2 from the north, and Michigan Highway 35, if you are coming from Lake Michigan. There is also a western approach using U.S. Highway 41; all

23 CEDAR RIVER PATHWAY

To US 2

To US 41

Cedar River

Loop 4
(7 miles)

Loop 3
(5 miles)

Loop 2
(3.5 miles)

River Road

Loop 1
(2 miles)

N

0   0.25   0.5
Miles

To MI 35

three access points use River Road (County Road 551) to reach the trailhead. It is easy to miss signs marking the turnoff to the trail and campground, so keep a sharp eye on your maps.

There are two trailheads for the pathway system. One is at a parking lot east of the Cedar River campground, and the other is at the edge of the campground on the Cedar River. Both are located off an access road west of River Rd.

The hike: From the campground, which is the start point for most hikers using the trail system, the **2-mile loop** moves quickly to the northeast, away from the river. About 0.4 mile from the trailhead hikers reach a junction with the 3.5-mile loop. This longer loop swings back toward the Cedar River, while the shorter loop swings east for nearly 0.3 miles to its return leg and junction for the second loop in the trail system. There is a bench located at the junction of these two trails, marking the halfway point. There are benches along the entire 7 miles of the trail, placed primarily for cross-country skiers but enjoyed every bit as much by hikers. Just past the bench the smallest loop swings south for the 0.5 mile trek to the access road leading into the campground. Once at the road, hikers will swing back west and use the roadway for the return trip to the campground and the trailhead. Although not a major thoroughfare, hikers are warned to keep their eyes open for traffic.

Loop two, the **3.5-mile loop**, offers a pleasant walk along the banks of the Cedar River. It picks up at the junction with the small loop mentioned above and presses northwest, making one small detour south before heading for the banks of the river. Another rest-stop bench is located on the riverbank, about 0.4 mile from the start of this second loop. From the bench, the trail continues on north for 0.2 mile to the outbound junction with the third loop, before bending east for another 0.2 mile to the inbound junction with that loop. Hikers on the 3.5-mile loop head south, then east, for 0.5 mile to a junction with the largest of the four loops, the 7-mile leg of the Cedar River Pathway. It is only about 0.3 mile from this junction to another junction with the first small loop.

Tracing loop three, the **5-mile loop** in this system, offers hikers nearly 0.75 mile of trail along the river. At the top of the loop, hikers swing briefly east away from the river to the outbound junction with the larger 7-mile loop in the system. From this junction, hikers head nearly due south for 0.7 mile to the junction with the 3.5-mile loop and the return trip to trailhead. You also have another option: if the river holds a special fascination for you, a right turn and 0.2-mile hike will take you back to the start point for the loop. Taking this route, you can trace the western edges of the pathway and stay along the riverbank for the return trip to the trailhead.

Loop four, the **7-mile pathway**, starts at the top of the 5-mile loop and heads generally east for 0.25 mile where the trail crosses River Road for the first time. After crossing the road the trail heads northeast for 0.75 mile to another trailside bench before swinging back to the southwest. About 0.75 mile later, the trail crosses River Rd. again, continuing for 0.25 mile to the junction with the return leg of the 3.5-mile loop in the system.

Hikers have several options at this point, depending on time and the condition of their tired feet. You can turn right at the junction and backtrack on the 3.5-mile loop to the river, then trace the river back to the campground. Or you can turn left and hike to the junction with the 2-mile loop, then make a right turn to backtrack on that trail to the campground. Another option is to simply keep bearing left through all the junctions and complete the long loop called the Cedar River Pathway.

There is one other lengthy detour that you could take: turn right at the outer end of the 7-mile loop, backtrack the 3.5-mile and 5-mile loops, and return to the campground by retracing your outbound trek along the river. Only time and energy limit the possibilities.

24   SENEY NATIONAL WILDLIFE REFUGE

Overview

The primary purpose of the vast Seney National Wildlife Refuge is the management of wildlife and its habitat. But included in the plan to preserve the area is an idea of balanced use, and that includes a variety of wildlife-oriented recreational opportunities. The refuge offers several clearly defined trails and roadways that offer the hiker 70 miles of possible loops and linear hikes to all corners of the area.

With the variety of food sources in the refuge, predators like this red fox are never at a loss for lunch.

The Seney National Wildlife Refuge is in a quiet corner of the eastern Upper Peninsula. The area permits visitors to peek into the marsh and wetland habitat so typical of the region. The refuge includes more than two dozen pools, several of which are artificially controlled to create nesting or feeding areas for a variety of waterfowl and birds common to the region. It is one of the few "wilderness" areas that permit vehicles, although these are limited to a 7-mile, self-guided marshland road that is also open to hikers and bikers. Nine of the pools in the refuge are open to fishing, but check local regulations before wetting a line.

The only scenic views here are those of the open pools and marsh grass flats; wildlife viewing is the main attraction. Visitors may see many species of birds, including waterfowl, loons, and raptors. Migrating ducks and geese use the refuge as a rest stop, but large numbers of Canada geese use the area as a nursery. Loons, sandhill cranes, trumpeter swans, eagles, and osprey also use the bounty of the refuge to feed their young. White-tailed deer, beaver, and otter are abundant in the area, but there are also black bear, coyote, bobcat, and three species of grouse in the confines of the refuge. The refuge hosts annual butterfly and wildflower outings.

Trails in the refuge are firm-surfaced, gravel routes that carve through the interior of the area and between pools. The 70 miles of road and trail give hikers the chance to customize a trek depending on how much time they have. No camping is permitted in the refuge, so plan hikes that allow for time to return to your vehicle for the trip back to the campground. There is no fresh water or other conveniences along the refuge trails.

The refuge is managed by the U.S. Fish & Wildlife Service, with its visitor center remaining open for much of the snow-free period, May through September.

General description: Wildlife refuge hikes for hikers at all levels of experience.
General location: 2 miles north of Germfask and 5 miles south of Seney in the central Upper Peninsula. The refuge is an easy hour's drive northwest of the Mackinac Bridge.
Maps: Visitor center staff provide an excellent map of the trails/roadways in the refuge. Markers along the routes make the hikes easy to follow.
Degree of difficulty: The short routes are easy family hikes. Longer routes, such as the Marshland Wildlife Route, are considered moderate because of length and the lack of services along the way.
Length: 70 miles of roadways and trails, on which hikers can create smaller linear walks and loops.
Elevations: The refuge is generally flat and marshy, as is much of the eastern U.P. The few ridges pose no problems for the casual hiker.
Special attractions: Wildlife viewing.
Best seasons: Spring and early summer have the most comfortable weather, but also swarm with biting insects. Fall is the most relaxing and least crowded time to visit the refuge—plus, waterfowl migration is in full gear, providing plenty of photo opportunities.

To Seney

To Germfask

77

J

I

H

F

G

E Pool

D

C Pool

C2 Pool

B Pool

A Pool

Sand Creek

Pine Creek

M2 Pool

Gray's Creek

Driggs River

Sand Creek

T2 Pool

Manistique River

Delta Creek

0   0.5   1
Miles

N

Large numbers of Canada geese use the refuge as a nursery each year.

For more information: Michael Tansy, Refuge Manager, Seney National Wildlife Refuge, HCR #2, Box 1, Seney, MI 49883, (906) 586-9851.

Finding the trailheads: There are several entrances to the refuge, but the common start point for hikes is the refuge visitor center, a short drive west of Michigan Highway 77. The paved road winds west from M-77 for 0.5 mile to the center and trailhead. Signs posted at the facility will direct hikers to the roadways and trails.

The hikes: The nearly 70 miles of well-developed forest roads in Seney National Wildlife Refuge provide limited access for vehicular traffic, and more access for bicyclists and hikers. The one trail set aside specifically for hikers is the 1.4-mile **Pine Ridge Nature Trail**, a walk along a portion of the dike system supporting several of the pools in the refuge. The trail is flat, wide, and well marked. It heads east from the visitor center and eventually traces the shores of a large pool that is home to Canada geese, loons, and a few trumpeter swans before returning to the start point.

Marshland Wildlife Drive is a 7-mile trip deeper into the heart of the refuge, offering visitors a look at a major part of the management system and diverse habitat within a wetland area. One-way vehicle traffic on the pathway insures that hikers won't be surprised by a car, but they will have to share the route. The first mile of path traces the southern shore of F Pool, climbing around the southern shoreline in several minor bumps before dropping back down to trace the eastern and southern shore of E Pool. To the uninitiated, it may seem that there are loons everywhere, but the most prominent flying creatures in the refuge are the small, biting variety! Plan to stop at the Swan Observation Deck and scan the pool for signs of waterfowl.

The most noticeable feature of the region is the wonderful earthy smell of the marsh that continuously surrounds you. The next portion of the Marshland Drive pathway stretches for 2 miles westward to its junction with the Fishing Loop. From here, the trail heads south along the eastern shore of D Pool, offering hikers a look from the Loon Observation Deck before swinging nearly due east for the final 4 miles to M-77.

Much of the remainder of the trip is spent passing between C and B pools, but make sure you stop at the Eagle Nest Observatory for a peek at an active eagle's nest on the far side of the pool. There are also plenty of ducks and geese on these two pools, along with wading shorebirds that nest along the grassy shores. Keep your eyes open for small mammals feeding in the shallows, and for the painted and snapping turtles that inhabit the pools.

Two other routes through the refuge are **Driggs River Road** and **Pine Creek Road**, both open to non-motorized traffic only. Driggs River Rd. is accessible from Michigan Highway 28, 7.5 miles west of Seney, but park managers recommend that you use the Marshland Wildlife Drive route to access this pathway at a junction point between D and C pools; this will also serve as access to Pine Creek Rd., a 10-mile linear pathway with two connector trails leading to the 18-mile trace of Driggs River Rd.

A good number of smaller loops and spur trails provide access to the remainder of the two dozen pools deep in the confines of the refuge. Although refuge officials recommend a side trip along a ridge or along the top of a dike to get a better view of wildlife and the many birds that call Seney home, remember that this is a wet and tangled environment that can quickly disorient a hiker.

25   FOX RIVER PATHWAY

Overview

Ernest Hemingway based his fabled "Big Two Hearted River" saga on his exploits along this classic northern Michigan trout stream. The trout fishing is still as good as it was when Hemingway visited the area, and the Fox River Pathway shadows the Fox and then the Little Fox rivers for nearly the entire length of its route from Seney to Kingston Lake Campground.

This is not an easy hike, but is instead a point-to-point trek that ends just 4 miles short of the Pictured Rocks National Lakeshore. Any hiker attempting the trek should be in good physical shape because of the nature of the terrain. You will need to allow extra time to rest feet and muscles if you intend to complete the hike in three or four days' time. Be sure to wear good boots to deal with the changing footing along the length of the route.

The trail parallels waterways for much of its length. It passes through stands of jack pine and the remnants of a boom-and-bust logging era that left its mark on the region, including the foundations of old logging camps, railroad

25   FOX RIVER PATHWAY

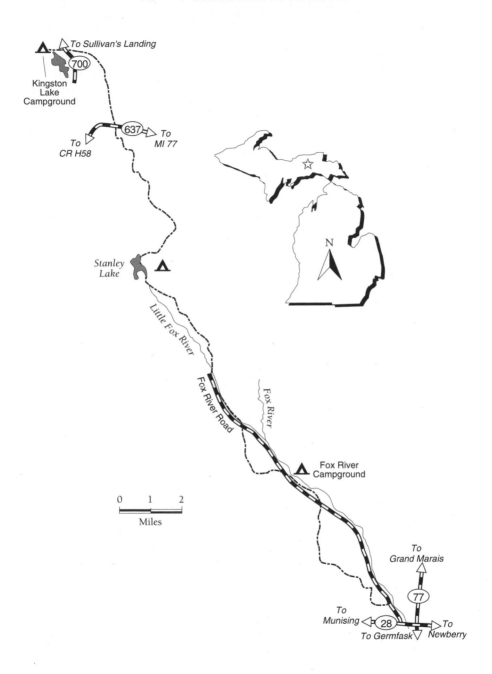

To Sullivan's Landing

700

Kingston
Lake
Campground

637
To CR H58
To MI 77

Stanley
Lake

Little Fox River

Fox River Road

Fox River

Fox River
Campground

0   1   2
Miles

To
Grand Marais

77

To Munising
28
To Germfask
To Newberry

N

grades long abandoned, and dams created to provide water for floating logs down to Seney. Forest fires finished the job of reseeding much of the area along the trail; the red pine plantations seen along the way were planted in the mid-1950s as part of an effort to plant more than 20 million pines in the Shingleton Forest Area. Although logging is the region's heritage, trout fishing in the Fox River attracts more people today. Wildlife abounds in the Singleton Forest and includes deer and black bear, as well as all sorts of small game and birdlife. In the fall, ducks and geese stop to use the river and the floodings along the system.

The trail opens up recreational opportunities in a large area. Hikers have several more trip options at its terminus, one of which is joining the North Country Trail. Keep in mind that this is a linear trail; hikers must make arrangements for transportation back to the trailhead or plan on retracing steps back to the start.

General description: A point-to-point trail through fabled Hemingway country near the Fox River.

General location: Near the community of Seney, 24 miles east of Munising in the Upper Peninsula.

Maps: The Department of Natural Resources office in Shingleton provides an excellent map and brochure on the trail system, complete with mile markers and other useful information.

Degree of difficulty: Moderate to difficult; not recommended for casual hikers.

Length: 27.5 miles from Seney to the Kingston Lake Campground.

Elevations: No difficult changes in terrain to deal with, but it might not seem that way after a long day.

Special attractions: Trout fishing in the Fox and Little Fox rivers, logging-era historic sites, wildlife.

Best season: Fall can be especially beautiful along the river and avoids earlier swarms of mosquitos and black flies, but be advised that hunters use the area starting in mid-September. If you are hiking during hunting season, wear bright clothing.

For more information: Area Forester, Shingleton Forest Area, Michigan Highway 28, Shingleton, MI 49884; District Forest Manager, Lake Superior State Forest, P.O. Box 445, Newberry, MI 49868.

Finding the trailhead: The trail begins at the Seney Township Campground, just north of the Fox River Bridge north of Seney on Michigan Highway 28. Once across the bridge, turn right on Fox River Road. The park is on the right, in about 0.25 mile.

The hike: The trail generally parallels the Fox River and the Little Fox River for the first 17 miles before heading cross-country the remaining 10 miles to Kingston Lake Campground. Between resting and fishing, hikers will find that the days slip by rather quickly.

From the Seney Township Campground, the trail heads west for 0.8 mile to the first of many stands of jackpine you will encounter along the trail. This

Black bear, although seldom seen, are present in numbers sufficient enough to warrant taking precautions around campsites.

stand extends for nearly 5 miles as you move along, then away from, the Fox River to navigate around blocks of private property. At Two Mile Ditch hikers swing back north and head once again for the river, slightly more than 3 miles away. The ditches here were dug just after the turn of the century as part of a plan to develop farms in the area; the plan failed, and the state assumed ownership of the land. At the end of this leg you will cross Fox River Rd. and enter the Fox River Plains, shadowing the rivers for the next 12 miles.

About 1 mile past the road crossing, you will find the first recommended stop along the trail, the Fox River Campground. Registration cards can be found on the information board at the entrance to campsites. You must register your campsite and remember to take out everything you carried in.

The next 2 miles of trail cross through a nearly 20-year-old cutting of mature jackpine. Hikers will pass the remnants of a logging camp built in the late 1880s, walking back into the rich history of the region. Since the lumber heyday, a total of 20 million trees have been planted in the Singleton Forest Area, a large portion of which grow along the flanks of the Fox River.

The trail crosses Fox River Rd. again, but this time follows the course of the Little Fox River northwest. Hikers must cross the river using an old truck trail. About 0.5 mile from the crossing, you will find one of eight water-control dams built along the Fox River system to regulate and store water for the loggers so they could float timber downstream to Seney. Nearly 2 miles farther, you will encounter a hill that was cut down so loggers could more easily move logs along an old sleigh road.

From here it's 4 miles to Stanley Lake Dam and the Stanley Lake Campground. Fishermen looking for a break from stream fishing can try their luck with the abundant northern pike in these slack waters. A 0.6-mile spur trail takes you along the shore of Stanley Lake, then right back to the pathway.

From here until the trail reaches Clyde Lake, 5 miles farther on, the terrain is a bit soggy as you pass through a series of berry bogs. The trail shadows the West Branch of the Fox River for a short time before heading back north. After passing Clyde, Fishhook, and Ewatt lakes, the trail crosses County Road 637. From the crossing it is 4.2 miles through the Kingston Plains and what locals refer to as a "stump museum," a collection of still-standing burned snags and stumps left behind by loggers in the late 1880s.

The trail swings west near the end to avoid private property and crosses County Road 700 just prior to entering the campground. If you continue north on CR 700 for 4 miles, you will reach the Pictured Rocks National Lakeshore's Twelve-Mile Beach Campground. Once there you can connect with the Pictured Rocks trail system. If you turn right at the campground, Grand Marais is only 11 miles away. Turn left to reach Munising in 24 miles.

26-35   SLEEPING BEAR DUNES NATIONAL LAKESHORE

Overview

The Sleeping Bear Dunes National Lakeshore is an area of stunning dunes, forests, and wetlands about 8 miles northeast of Glen Arbor in central Leelanau County, between Lake Michigan and the north shore of Little Traverse Lake. The Sleeping Bear Dunes region is a multi-use area and, except for riders of mechanized devices, open to everyone with a desire to explore the dunes along the Lake Michigan shoreline. The entire area was submerged under ancestral Lake Michigan about 11,000 years ago and has gradually emerged. The Chippewa Indians gave birth to the legends that created the Sleeping Bear name.

Low ridges along the shoreline are punctuated by wetlands. Loops and connector trails within the area offer an all-day outing or a quick look at the landscape of the countryside and offshore islands, including North and South Manitou islands. Few trails in the park are long enough to fill an entire day, but each trail listed below offers a different look at the mix of environments.

Most trails are easily handled by even the casual hiker, but the sandy trails throughout the area can be tough on feet if you have ill-fitting shoes or boots. On trails along the Sleeping Bear Dunes, heavy hiking boots should be left behind in favor of the new lightweight boots or high-top sneakers.

General description: A short loop through diverse habitats—dunes, forests, wetlands, and shore.
General location: Sleeping Bear Dunes National Lakeshore.
Maps: National Park Service area map.
Degree of difficulty: Easy, but sandy portions of the route can be tough to walk on.
Length: 2.8 miles.
Elevations: Low ridges and dunes created by blowing and shifting sand make things interesting near the start of the loop, but the remainder is fairly flat and presents no special challenges.
Special attractions: A unique opportunity to visit the lakeshore of the Sleeping Bear Dunes. Wetlands and small creeks here support wildlife and birds amid plenty of opportunities to view the nature of the dunes.
Best season: Midsummer to late summer, for two basic reasons: warm temperatures and a decided lack of bugs. The blazing autumn color draws visitors, but hunters are in the area at the same time.
For more information: Sleeping Bear Dunes National Lakeshore, P.O. Box 277, 9922 Front Street, Empire, MI 49630, (616) 326-5134.
Finding the trailhead: From Glen Arbor, drive north 8 miles on Michigan

Hikers should come prepared for varying trail conditions, especially the sandy footing so prevalent in the shoreline areas. National Park Service photo.

26 GOOD HARBOR BAY LOOP

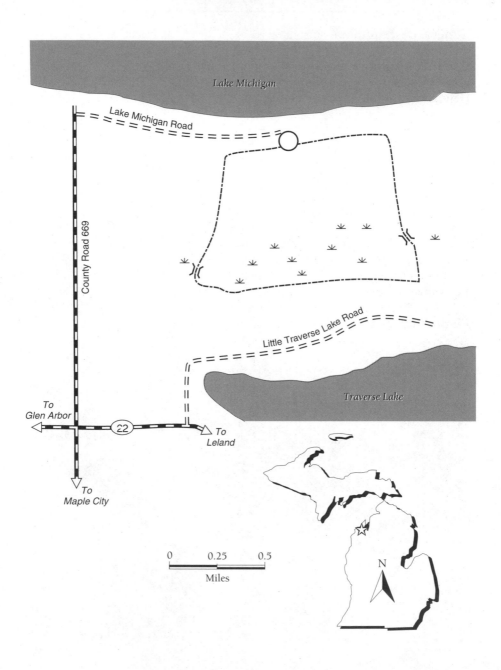

Highway 22 to County Road 669. Turn left on CR 669 and go for 1.5 miles to Lake Michigan Road, then turn right and continue for 1 mile to the trailhead, on the right.

The hike: The 2.8-mile Good Harbor Bay Loop traces more of a square than a meandering circle. It moves through sandy dunes and wooded fringe areas, then into a wetland habitat that borders the southern leg of the trail, then woodlands, and, finally, the sand shores of Lake Michigan again. The four sides of this "loop" are each about 0.75 mile long, with the trailhead located midway along the northern leg.

From the trailhead, the trail heads east through the dunes that make the region so attractive to visitors. This is the toughest part of the trail, since footing can be unstable on nothing more than shifting sand. The trail goes east for about 0.4 mile, then turns south, moving out of the dunes and into a forested area for nearly 0.5 mile before giving way to the wettest area of the loop.

Hikers will cross a small footbridge over a ribbon of water as they head for the next corner of the trail. The trail switches back to the west about 1 mile into the wetlands. This stretch of the trail is especially interesting during the spring—not because of insects but because of the diverse wildflowers found along the trail. At the end of this leg is a short boardwalk that carries hikers across the wettest section.

The western leg of the trail swings due north for about 0.6 mile through a forested area that offers shade in summer and a look at the backbone of the entire dunes area.

At the end of this leg, the trail swings due east for the final few hundred yards to the trailhead. The picnic area east of the trailhead is a terrific spot to rest those weary feet and relax before moving on to the next trail in the Sleeping Bear Dunes.

27   PYRAMID POINT LOOP

General description: A 2.8-mile loop with spectacular vistas through what is probably the most remote corner of the park.
General location: Sleeping Bear Dunes National Lakeshore.
Maps: Pyramid Point Trail Map, provided free of charge at the visitor center; USGS Glen Arbor quad.
Degree of difficulty: Moderate. Like other sandy trails in the Sleeping Bear Dunes National Lakeshore, the hike is rated such because of the footing and, in this case, shifts in terrain. Proper-fitting boots or shoes are essential.
Length: 2.8 miles.
Elevations: Lookout Point, 840 feet, and several steep climbs or descents of 125 feet or more.
Special attractions: Lookout Point, from which hikers can see the shipwreck of the Morazan, South Manitou Island and its lighthouse, North Manitou

27 PYRAMID POINT LOOP

Island, the Manitou Shoals, South Fox Island, and Pyramid Point, as well as a great view of the surrounding country. This is a favorite launch site for hang glider pilots.

Best season: Spring through fall. Be aware of hunters from mid-September through November.

For more information: Sleeping Bear Dunes National Lakeshore, P.O. Box 277, 9922 Front Street, Empire, MI 49630, (616) 326-5134.

Finding the trailhead: From Glen Arbor, head north for 5 miles. As Michigan Highway 22 turns east, make a left turn onto Port Oneida Road. Continue on this road for about 2 miles, then turn right onto Basch Road. The dirt road leads to the parking lot and trailhead in about 300 yards.

The hike: The Pyramid Point Loop blends all the various environments that make up the Sleeping Bear Dunes National Lakeshore with spectacular vistas as far as the eye can see.

From the trailhead, the hike meanders toward the sandy shoreline of Lake Michigan along a deserted two-track road and over glacial moraines that have given root to a beech and maple forest. The trees act as barriers against winds off the open lake. The hike for the first few hundred yards is through a fairly level meadow, but the trail begins to climb as you near the trees.

For the next 0.25 mile the climb becomes more noticeable as you enter a mixed grove of hardwoods that, in summer, provides a bit of shade and in fall is ablaze with color. About midway through this forest belt is a trail junction; a short, 0.2-mile spur path leads to Lookout Point, a spectacular vantage point used as a hang glider launch site. The hike is decidedly uphill and the footing is not all that stable, but the trek is worth it.

After you take in the phenomenal view, retrace your steps to the junction and head east for 0.6 mile to the next posted junction in the trail. From here hikers have the option of shortening the loop by nearly a mile, or continuing on the complete loop through this quiet corner of the dunes area. The main trail drops more than 100 feet in elevation, eventually breaking out of the trees and into another large meadow. The trail swings southeast from the junction, through the meadow, then back northwest toward the trailhead. Only about 0.25 mile of the loop passes through open meadow. Hikers re-enter the trees for the 0.6-mile leg to Basch Rd. The final 0.4 mile back to the trailhead is a walk along Basch Rd.; hikers should keep an eye out for traffic.

28   BAY VIEW HIKING TRAILS

General description: Trails through mature beech and maple forests in the southern portion of the national lakeshore system, with views to the north. The dunes are at the feet of hikers once they reach Lookout Point.
General location: Sleeping Bear Dunes National Lakeshore.
Maps: National Park Service area map.
Degree of difficulty: Moderate, due to the length and changeable footing of several portions of trail.
Length: 9 miles, divided into shorter loops: Lookout Point Trail, 2.3 miles; Meadow Trail, 1.1 miles; and the High Trail and Low Trail, 5-6 miles each, which share much of the same pathways. Hikers can customize treks through the system to match available time and interests.
Elevations: Hilly, but not too challenging for hikers who take their time.

Special attractions: Lookout Point, and related views.
Best season: Midsummer, since warm temperatures make hiking comfortable and the availability of shoreline a real plus. Early fall attracts visitors because of the color, and hunters ply the woodlands for upland birds; archers are present from October 1 until the start of the firearm deer season in mid-November.

For more information: Sleeping Bear Dunes National Lakeshore, P.O. Box 277, 9922 Front Street, Empire, MI 49630, (616) 326-5134.

Finding the trailheads: Bay View trails are accessible from two trailheads. To reach the Thorson trailhead, go 4 miles north of Glen Arbor on M-22. At Thorson Road, turn left and go 0.5 mile to the trailhead, on the left. To find the Homestead trailhead, go just 2 miles north of Glen Arbor on M-22 to Homestead Resort. The trailhead is just north of the resort on the right side of the road.

The hikes: The Bay View Hiking Trail is one of the longer trails in the Sleeping Bear Dunes National Lakeshore, made up of four separate loops. The northernmost loop provides an outstanding view of the Lake Michigan shoreline and several offshore islands. The trail offers a mix of environments, including mature forests and the sandy dunes that give the area its name and appeal. Trailheads at opposite ends of the trail offer convenient access to visitors arriving from north or south. All loops are accessible from either of the trailheads.

The most popular loop in the system is the **Lookout Point Loop**, a 2.4-mile trail to the north of the Thorson Trailhead. The trail leads through a series of low sandy hills and open grassy areas that set the mood for the lakeshore and its namesake, but none of the obstacles are considered more than moderate in difficulty. From the trailhead, the trail heads north for 0.4 mile to the junction with a 0.1-mile spur trail to the lookout. Once atop the lookout, you will have . . . on a clear day . . . a view of South Manitou Island and its lighthouse, North Manitou Island, the Manitou Shoals Beacon, South Fox Island, and Pyramid Point. Returning to the loop, hikers will head north for about 0.1 mile before turning decidedly east and heading that way for nearly 1 mile. Then the trail shadows M-22, crosses Thorson Road, and heads back to the trailhead. According to park officials, this loop is not only the most popular in the Bay View system, but also the least confusing.

The other three main loops in the system, **Meadow Trail, High Trail,** and **Low Trail**, offer configurations that allow hikers to customize treks to match timetables. These loops, with the exception of the Meadow Trail, can be confusing; refer to your map often to remain on the trail you intend to follow. Finding yourself 3 or 4 miles from where you thought you were, with no water and sore feet, is not a pleasant climax to a great day on the trails.

The southern half of the three loops south of the Thorson trailhead offer some shade in mixed hardwood forest, but trails are still sandy and footing isn't all that solid. The three southern loops range in length from 2 to 2.5 miles and, according to park officials, offer more options than one could hike in a weekend. Combining portions of the various loops will create a hike that easily fits into a days' outing and doesn't tax your enthusiasm to the point of apathy. Two recommended hikes: combine portions of the Meadow Loop and High Trail or, for a longer hike, combine the High and Low trails.

The first loop is a 4-mile hike through the southern end of the trail system; the extended hike is a 4.5-mile hike through the length of the system, and can easily be combined with a visit to Lookout Point at the north end of the loop. From the Homestead trailhead, both trails share the same 0.2-mile start, taking hikers on an easterly heading to reach the main pathways.

For the **Meadow-High Trails Loop**: Turn left at the 0.2-mile junction and make a snakelike meander for 0.5 mile to the first of three connector trails that only seem to serve to confuse many hikers. Advice from park officials: stay to the left. The first two connector trails, 0.1 and 0.2 mile long respectively, provide shortcuts to the return leg of this 4-mile loop. At a junction with a 0.1-mile spur trail, the main pathway bears to the left, looping 1 mile through a mix of forest and open sandy fields. That loop returns to the main pathway at the junction with the spur-trail shortcut and bends east for the 0.3-mile hike to the junction with the High Trail. The Meadow-High Trails loop then turns south for 0.5 mile, then follows Thorson Road for the next 0.6 mile. Watch the right side of the roadway for the signs pointing the way back to the Homestead trailhead. From the signs, the hike swings back west for 0.4 mile to the spur trail back to the trailhead.

The **High-Low Trails Loop**: This loop retraces the final 1.7 miles of the Meadow-High Trails Loop, actually backtracking to the point where Meadow Trail joins the High Trail. Just beyond this point the trees give way to meadows and stretches of sand; the trail meanders over low hills. The junction with the first connector trail appears on the right, just 0.2 mile from the junction with Meadow Trail; this 0.2-mile spur leads to the return leg along the Low Trail. From this point it is another 0.6 mile to the Thorson trailhead, which is a good choice for hikers looking to enjoy the full scenic beauty of the Sleeping Bear Dunes National Lakeshore. From here, you can either turn right and link up with the Low Trail and thus begin the hike back to the Homestead trailhead, or take the time to hike the 2.4-mile loop that will carry you to Lookout Point. I recommend the diversion. The view is magnificent.

From the Thorson trailhead, the return leg starts with a short 0.1-mile hike to the junction with the return leg of the Lookout Point loop. The trail then heads south for 0.4 mile to the eastern end of the connector trail mentioned earlier, and continues for 0.9 mile to the junction with Thorson Road. The final 0.6 mile of the High-Low Trails Loop retraces a portion of the start of the hike, crossing Thorson Road, then returns along the spur trail to the trailhead.

29 ALLIGATOR HILL TRAILS

General description: Hiking and cross-country skiing trails in the inland portion of Sleeping Bear Dunes National Lakeshore.

General location: Sleeping Bear Dunes National Lakeshore.

Maps: National Park Service area map.

Degree of difficulty: "Green" loop, easy; "Blue" loop, moderate; "Black" loop, challenging. Ratings posted along the trails are there for cross-country skiers, but only generally reflect the hazards for hikers.

Length: 8.3 miles total; "Green," "Blue," and "Black" loops are each about 2.5 miles long, and a 0.8-mile spur trail to a scenic overlook in the center of the "Blue" loop.

Trails throughout the region guide hikers through a variety of habitats. National Park Service photo.

Elevations: Relatively flat along the "Green" loop, rolling hills on the "Blue" loop, and more challenging climbs and descents on the "Black" loop.

Special attractions: An off-shore trail system offering a unique look at the "rest of the story" of Sleeping Bear Dunes National Lakeshore. Glacial terrain, upland and wetland habitats, wildlife, and, in season, carpets of wildflowers.

Best season: Fall rates highest among the choices for hikers; the loops are groomed cross-country ski trails when winter arrives, so they won't be available during the coldest months.

For more information: Sleeping Bear Dunes National Lakeshore, P.O. Box 277, 9922 Front Street, Empire, MI 49630, (616) 326-5134.

Finding the trailheads: The trails are northeast of Little Glen Lake, 2 miles west of Glen Arbor and 7 miles northeast of Empire. From Empire, go north 9 miles on Michigan Highway 109 to Stocking Road, then turn right and go 1 mile to the trailhead on the left. Stocking Road is just east of the entrance to D.H. Day Campground on M-109.

The hike: The Alligator Hill system is one of the few trail systems in the park that does not provide a panoramic view of the lakeshore. But these inland trails are just as important in understanding the complete picture of the Sleeping Bear region, offering a look into the nature of the region that was also carved by retreating glaciers and years of wear from lakeshore breezes and Michigan winters. The trails weave through a mixture a field and forest habitats that attract large numbers of birds and other wildlife. In springtime, the trails are bordered by a rich mixture of wildflowers.

This three-loop trail system has been developed as a hiking-skiing system. Each of its teardrop-shaped trail loops is 2.5 miles long, and the "Blue" trail has an added 0.8-mile spur trail to a patch of high ground that affords a limited view of the surrounding area. The trails are all well marked and easy to follow. The "Green" and "Blue" trails should be hiked in a counterclockwise direction, while it's recommended that the "Black" loop be followed clockwise.

From the trailhead off Stocking Road, hikers must start all loops on a portion of the "Green" loop. This easy loop heads north for approximately 0.25 mile before turning east for the mile-long hike to the junction with the "Blue" loop. Both loops turn south at this point, sharing the next 0.2 mile of trail. About 100 yards down the trail is the junction with the spur trail leading off to the left toward the scenic lookout mentioned earlier. This 0.8-mile linear trail ends at a high point in the center of the loop formed by the "Blue" trail and provides a good, but limited view of the surrounding countryside. Back on the main train, the two loops soon split, with the "Green" trail heading generally westward back toward the trailhead, 1.1 miles from this fork in the trail. About 0.8 mile from the end of the trail, hikers will pass the junction with the "Black" trail feeding in from the left. From here it's only 0.3 mile back to the trailhead.

To reach the "Blue" loop, hikers must first hike the outward, or northern leg, of the "Green" trail past the spur trail leading to the scenic lookout, heading south to the fork in the trail. Here, hikers will take the left fork and head southeast for nearly 1 mile. About 0.35 mile along this leg of the trail, hikers will pass the junction with the outbound leg of the "Black" loop trail that heads south from this point. From this junction, the pathway continues east for 0.65 mile before swinging north. The trail continues toward Lake Michigan for 0.4 mile before turning west for the 1-mile hike back to the junction of the two loops. Here, hikers have two options: one, head back to the trailhead by backtracking along the northern leg of the "Green" loop; or two, retrace the 0.2 mile of trail shared by the two loops, then follow the southern leg of the "Green" loop back to the trailhead. Either way, hikers will have to use the first loop to get back to the trailhead.

The final, more difficult loop, is another 2.5-mile trail system that features more hills and valleys to be negotiated. It is a less difficult task for hikers than skiers, but challenging nonetheless. To reach the start of the "Black" route, hikers must first trace the first half of the "Green" route, the shared pathway, and 0.35 mile of the southern leg of the "Blue" trail. Once at the junction, hikers head south for 0.9 mile, turn west for another 0.9 mile, and then go north for 0.6 mile to a junction with the return leg of the "Green" trail leading back to the trailhead.

30 DUNES HIKING TRAILS

General description: A challenging point-to-point Dune Climb-Dunes Trail for adventurous hikers, and a more gentle loop at Sleeping Bear Point for less-experienced dune fans.

General location: Sleeping Bear Dunes National Lakeshore.

Maps: National Park Service Dunes Hiking Trail map; USGS Glen Haven quad.

Degree of difficulty: Moderate to difficult for even experienced hikers, since loose sand makes walking strenuous.

Length: Two trails—a 4-mile point-to-point trail requiring about 4 hours to complete, and a 2.8-mile loop near the Maritime Museum adjacent to Sleeping Bear Point.

Elevations: The one demanding elevation in the area is at the start of the point-to-point trail. The nearly 150-foot-high dune is a 50-degree scramble up through shifting sand. There are several other dunes to scale, but none with the challenge of that first dune.

Special attractions: Dune Climb, Maritime Museum.

Best season: Late summer and early fall are favorite times, but don't overlook the Dunes Trail as a spring destination. The stubborn vegetation puts on a brief, beautiful show in the spring.

For more information: Sleeping Bear Dunes National Lakeshore, P.O. Box 277, 9922 Front Street, Empire, MI 49630, (616) 326-5134.

Finding the trailheads: The Dune Climb trailhead is about 6 miles from the National Park Service Visitor Center at the junction of Michigan Highways 72 and 22 in Empire. From the center, take M-22 north to Michigan Highway 109. Signs will direct you to the Dune Climb. The loop trailhead is located near the Maritime Museum off Michigan Highway 209. To reach this trailhead, continue north from the Dune Climb trailhead to the M-109/M-209 junction. Continue north on M-209 for about 1.5 miles to the signs marking the trail.

The hikes: The Dune Climb-Dunes Trail is a point-to-point hike of nearly 4 miles that requires at least 4 hours to complete; the 2.8-mile loop at Sleeping Bear Point is a relaxing hike through much the same habitat but without the dramatic changes in elevations.

The **Dunes Trail** is the most popular of all the trail systems in the Sleeping Bear National Lakeshore because of the nearly 150-foot **Dune Climb** at the start of the point-to-point trail. There are few trees here, but the grasses, wildflowers, and occasional windswept tree make this a starkly beautiful area. The sandy shoreline of Lake Michigan and the panorama of the dunes environment make this an unforgettable hike.

The trail begins only a few yards from the parking lot off M-109, which is probably the last solid footing you will have for the next 4 hours. Ascending the dune in front of you will test your resolve and remind you that you have knees and thigh muscles in need of conditioning. Take your time climbing the dune because you have a long way to go; even though the next few dunes don't demand the same kind of climb, they will still be taxing.

The top of this first dune rises about 890 feet above sea level. From there, the first of the blue trail markers will be visible, as will the next dune to conquer. Atop the next dune hikers get their first look at the welcome waters of Lake Michigan, still a ways off. The trail signpost indicates 1 mile to go, but there are a few climbs left before you can cool your feet in the lake. In this

30 DUNES HIKING TRAILS

Lake Michigan

2.8 Mile Loop

209

To Glen Arbor

109

3.5 Mile Round Trip

N

0   0.5   1
Miles

To Empire

dune environment, the only things to break the monotony of sand are patches of tough beach grass. The footing is tough.

From the last big dune hikers will get a treat: a view of South Manitou Island with its historic 120-year-old lighthouse. From the top of this last tall dune, it's only about 0.5 mile to the shore of Lake Michigan. The trail offers no loops back to the trailhead, so you must retrace your steps.

The **loop trail at Sleeping Bear Point** is a more leisurely walk through the sandy environment that has made Sleeping Bear Dunes National Lakeshore such a popular stop for tourists and hikers. The trail is well marked and offers no real challenge for even the casual hiker, although it is still a sandy trail and walking can be tough on poorly protected feet. Vegetation is not quite as sparse as on the Dune Climb trail, but it still isn't sufficient to provide a lot of solid footing.

Springtime in this corner of the system can be picturesque, since wildflowers tough enough to survive the windswept nature of the area provide a colorful backdrop for the stark sand dunes.

31   SHAUGER HILL HIKING TRAIL

General description: A 2.4-mile trail through beech and maple hardwood forests, fields, and pine plantations. One of the few trails in the National Lakeshore system that do not provide a view of the dunes.
General location: Sleeping Bear Dunes National Lakeshore.
Maps: National Park Service Shauger Hill Hiking Trail map.
Degree of difficulty: Moderate, because of changing terrain and several uphill climbs and steep descents.
Length: Just 2.4 miles, but seems longer due to the terrain.
Elevations: The changes in terrain are all uphill during the first half of the hike and steeply downhill in the latter half of the trek. None of the elevations are drastic, but can be tiring, especially for the casual hiker in a hurry.
Special attractions: This rich woodland supports a variety of life dependent on the changing seasons, with wildflowers and morels abundant in spring, songbirds and shade in summer, and vivid foliage in fall.
Best season: Summer to fall. Much of the park is open to hunting; if you hike after September 15, wear bright clothing and stay on the trails.
For more information: Sleeping Bear Dunes National Lakeshore, P.O. Box 277, 9922 Front Street, Empire, MI 49630, (616) 326-5134.
Finding the trailhead: From Empire, drive north on Michigan Highway 109 for 3.5 miles to the entrance for Scenic Drive on the left. The trailhead and parking area are located about 0.5 mile from the junction.

The hike: The Shauger Hill Hiking Trail is one of the few trails in the park that don't provide a view of the famous dunes that give the region its name. This inland trail loop provides a look at the "other" side of the dunes area: the forests that hold it all in place along the Lake Michigan shoreline.

Hikers set out from the trailhead in a southerly direction, heading clockwise to cross Scenic Drive in just a few yards. The next landmark is the crossing of Shauger Hill Road. From here it's on into the beech and maple forest that dominates the landscape.

The trail winds through the forested area for nearly a mile before crossing Shauger Hill Rd. for the last time as the trail turns back north for the final 1.4 miles to the trailhead. The trail is well marked and easy to follow as it snakes its way back to the start point. There are a number of steep downhill stretches along this segment of the trail, so take your time as you head back to the car.

The final 200 yards of the loop are reached after the second crossing of Scenic Drive. From here, it's an easy walk south back to the trailhead. Although not a long trail, Shauger Hill Hiking Trail offers a different perspective on Sleeping Bear Dunes National Lakeshore. Plan on including this hike in a day's adventuring in the region.

General description: A hike through both natural and manmade habitats.
General location: Sleeping Bear Dunes National Lakeshore.
Maps: National Park Service area map.
Degree of difficulty: Easy.
Length: 1.5 miles.
Elevations: No challenges; reaching the Windy Moraine scenic overlook won't tax the casual hiker.
Special attractions: Diversity, including human structures reclaimed by natural progression, stands of large trees, and birds and animals of all sizes.
Best season: Fall, but be aware that hunters use these tracts of public land when small and big game seasons open mid-September.
For more information: Sleeping Bear Dunes National Lakeshore, P.O. Box 277, 9922 Front Street, Empire, MI 49630, (616) 326-5134.
Finding the trailhead: From Empire, drive north on Michigan Highway 109 for 4 miles to the junction with Welch Road. Here, turn right for the last few hundred yards to the entrance of the trailhead parking area.

The hike: This loop is a short excursion and an easy one, but is meant to be combined with the other trails in the Sleeping Bear Dunes National Lakeshore area to create a longer stay in this scenic portion of the Lower Peninsula. The

The view from the bluffs along the Lake Michigan shoreline are well worth all the effort made to reach them. National Park Service photo.

32 WINDY MORAINE LOOP

trail makes a great diversion from the sandy loops nearer to the Lake Michigan shoreline and provides unique photo opportunities.

The first 0.75 mile will expose hikers to a rich diversity of habitats, both naturally occurring and manmade. Fields, forests, and buffer zones all are present along this half of the loop. Remnants of an old farm are marked by a few remaining apple trees. About 0.25 mile from the trailhead, you will find the decaying reminder that a sawmill once operated here: slab wood, decomposing, which feeds a whole community of forest life. About 0.5 mile from the trailhead, a large sugar maple provides a welcome respite from the heat of summer. It's a comfortable spot to reflect on whatever is on your mind.

From this point on to Windy Moraine Overlook, be on the lookout for wildlife of all sorts, including squirrels, raccoons, and even deer. The Windy Moraine Overlook is the halfway point in the loop, and from here you will be able to see a large portion of the Sleeping Bear Dunes National Lakeshore.

From the overlook, the trail heads north and then west back toward the trailhead. The final landmark is a pine plantation about 0.25 mile from the end of the trail.

33   OLD INDIAN TRAILS

General description: Loop trails founded by American Indians, winding through mature stands of trees to the shore.

General location: At the southern edge of Sleeping Bear Dunes National Lakeshore.

Maps: National Park Service Old Indian Trail map; USGS Frankfort quad.

Degree of difficulty: Easy, but make sure you are wearing good shoes or boots on sandy trails near the lakeshore.

Length: Inner loop, 2.25 miles; outer loop, 2.3 miles.

Elevations: Minor. The few low dunes crossed just before the shoreline pose no problems for the casual hiker.

Special attractions: Isolated beaches along Lake Michigan, and a sprinkling of wildflowers in wooded areas.

Best seasons: Summer and early fall.

For more information: Sleeping Bear Dunes National Lakeshore, P.O. Box 277, 9922 Front Street, Empire, MI 49630, (616) 326-5134.

Finding the trailhead: The trailhead is approximately 12 miles south of the National Park Visitor Center, off Michigan Highway 22. Watch for the signs on the right. If heading north from Frankfort on M-22, the entrance is just past the M-22/Sutter Road junction, on the left.

The hike: The two loops of this trail follow the crests of tree-covered ancient dunes, well inland from today's shoreline. The dunes mark the post-glacial shoreline of Lake Michigan. The mix of hardwoods and pines that cover the area provide welcome relief from summer heat. The trail is a portion of an Indian trail used to reach the shore area to fish and camp.

Once out of the parking lot at the trailhead, hikers are swallowed up by the hardwood and pine forest that covers much of the first sections of the trail. You will pass a junction with the return leg of the trail about 150 yards from the trailhead. Continue north past the junction with the middle trail to a point 0.3 mile from the start point where the trail takes a decided westward tack.

For the next 1.2 miles you will work your way over a series of low dunes covered with vegetation and pass through beech, maple, and oak forest. There are a few low-lying wet areas that break the tree cover, but for the most part

33 OLD INDIAN TRAILS

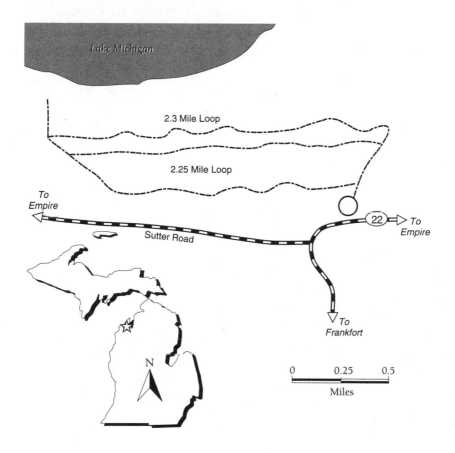

you will remain in the forest until you break out onto the beach.

At the end of the westward leg you will reach a marker indicating the path to the shoreline of Platte Bay. The short spur is only 0.3 mile long, but the sandy trail here makes hiking more difficult. Once at the lakeshore you will be able to see both North and South Manitou islands, the famous Sleeping Bear Dune, and miles of unspoiled beaches to the east.

Returning to the junction, head southeast past the junction with the middle trail for nearly 0.25 mile to where the return leg of the Old Indian Trail heads easterly. The trek back to the trailhead is about 0.75 mile.

The center, or middle, trail splits the outer loop through the middle of the wooded area surrounding this system. It provides an interesting diversion. Take it, then turn right at the junction with the outbound leg. You will reach the trailhead in just a matter of minutes.

General description: A picturesque, point-to-point hike with a final panorama that has caused many hikers to turn an hour's hike into an all-day outing to the 400-foot-high bluffs overlooking Lake Michigan.

General location: Sleeping Bear Dunes National Lakeshore.

Maps: National Park Service Empire Bluff Trail map; USGS Empire quad.

Degree of difficulty: Moderate, because of the changes in terrain and sandy trails.

Length: 2 miles round-trip.

Elevations: The terrain is hilly, so anticipate short, gentle climbs.

Special attractions: The best 2-mile hike in Michigan. Six interpretive stations look into the history of the area, but the bluffs and the spectacular view they provide are the focus of the hike.

Best season: Spring through early fall, since winter's blasts off Lake Michigan can be downright frigid. On a warm winter day, the view from the bluff is quite spectacular.

For more information: Sleeping Bear Dunes National Lakeshore, P.O. Box 277, 9922 Front Street, Empire, MI 49630, (616) 326-5134.

Finding the trailheads: From the National Park Visitor Center, head south on Michigan Highway 22 for 2 miles to the junction with Wilco Road. Turn left. The trailhead is 1 mile down the road, on the left.

The hike: Empire Bluff is rated by many as the best 2-mile hike anywhere in the state of Michigan. The hike is not difficult, and the rewards along the route are similar to those reserved for hikers who endure much more difficult systems. The hike is interrupted by six interpretive stations and a spectacular view at the outer end of the trail, revealing much of Sleeping Bear Dunes National Lakeshore, Platte Bay, and, 7 miles offshore, South Manitou Island.

Hikers get a taste of hilly terrain right from the start. A boulder left behind by a receding glacier some 12,000 years ago marks the first of the six interpretive sites. From here hikers will pass through open fields and past farm equipment left behind from an era long gone by. The soils weren't rich enough to support many crops, but hay farmers eked out a living from this area until about the mid-1940s. Leaving the fields, hikers move into a mature beech and maple forest. The trail here is fairly level. During summer, hikers will enjoy the shade of the forest and a sprinkling of wildflowers.

The hilly nature of the Empire Bluff Trail reappears once again as hikers move into an area called the Old Orchard. This isn't actually an orchard, but trees may have grown from fruit discarded in the area; there is a grove of fruit trees here. The remains of small American yew once plentiful in the area are the focus of interpretive site five, the lead-in for the spectacular vista waiting just ahead.

A short climb to station six and the Empire Bluff Overlook reveals a breathtaking view of the park and its miles of shoreline. The trail swings south, following a boardwalk for 500 feet to an observation deck.

Hikers will want to spend time at the vista, then will have to retrace their steps to the trailhead.

35 PLATTE PLAINS TRAILS

General description: A 13-mile trail system divided into three shorter loops. Dune scenery highlights these relatively easy lakeshore hikes through rolling terrain.
General location: Sleeping Bear Dunes National Lakeshore.
Maps: National Park Service Platte Plains Trail map; USGS Beulah quad.
Degree of difficulty: Easy.
Length: 13 miles of trails, broken into loops of 3.6, 4.5, and 6 miles.
Elevations: No challenge.
Special attractions: Scenic overlooks along Lake Michigan; abundant wildlife.
Best season: Midsummer to early fall. Spring can be buggy, given the

number of low areas along the eastern edge of the system.

For more information: Sleeping Bear Dunes National Lakeshore, P.O. Box 277, 9922 Front Street, Empire, MI 49630, (616) 326-5134.

Finding the trailheads: To reach the north trailhead, head south from Empire on Michigan Highway 22 for 3.5 miles until you reach Esch Road. Turn right; the trailhead is in 1 mile. To reach the central trailhead, go south 1.5 miles from the Esch Rd. junction, and watch for the sign on the right for Trails End Road. The trailhead is 0.5 mile from the turn. The southern trailhead is in the Platte River Campground. Drive south of the Trails End Rd. junction for 4 miles to Lake Michigan Road. Turn right and follow the signs to the campground on the right.

The hike: The Platte River Campground is a popular stop for summer users of the Sleeping Bear Dunes area, but few venture out on the trails, leaving hikers a bit of solitude and the beauty of the Lake Michigan shoreline. This trail system also has a remote wilderness campground, with no water, sources of food, or heavy foot–traffic to spoil your adventure. The loops of the trail system allow for plenty of time to explore the varied environments found along these trails. Lakes, streams, and the full range of dry habitats make a visit to the Platte Plains Trail a constantly changing adventure.

Leaving the Platte River Campground (the southern trailhead), hikers enter a pine thicket that masks rolling terrain. The trees open up on sand dunes along the shoreline of Lake Michigan about 0.5 mile from the trailhead. The soft, sandy trail makes walking a little strenuous, but it ends soon, so just slow down a bit.

From a junction with the first of three trails to scenic overlooks, the trail turns east and begins to parallel the shoreline, crossing Peterson Road in 0.5 mile. A second scenic overlook can be reached by turning left on Peterson Rd. and hiking a few hundred yards to the lake. It is about 1 mile from the Peterson Road crossing to the final overlook site; to get there, hikers will pass through mixed hardwoods and pine.

Beyond the third overlook, after nearly 1 mile of gently rolling terrain, hikers reach the remote White Pine Campground. The campground is set between wooded ridges and only contains six sites. Everything you need will have to be carried in and out of this beautiful little campsite.

From the campground, the loop continues southeast for 0.8 mile to the first junction with the 3.6-mile loop. The trail takes a decidedly southern tack, making a 1.1-mile leg to the southern junction with the smallest loop in the Platte Plains system. About 0.3 mile past this junction, hikers cross Lasso Road, continuing west for a 2-mile trek back to the second crossing of Peterson Rd. Hikers continue west, then turn north for the 0.3-mile hike to a signpost that will direct you back to the Platte River Campground.

The shortest loop, which connects the trailhead from Trails End Rd. (the central trailhead) with the main loop, shares 1.1 miles of the bigger loop's eastern leg. The trail meanders through wooded and wet areas, eventually following a portion of the western shoreline of Deer Lake before returning to the Trails End Road trailhead.

The 4.5-mile loop from Esch Rd. can also be started at the Trails End Road

35 PLATTE PLAINS TRAILS

entry point. This trail loop follows a course around Otter Lake, then follows the course of Otter Creek to Lake Michigan and back again. This wet section of trail presents the problem of keeping feet dry, but the variety of wildlife found in this area will distract you from sodden feet.

36   OCQUEOC FALLS
BICENTENNIAL PATHWAY

General description: Trails near Lower Michigan's largest waterfall, on the Ocqueoc River.

General location: 11 miles west of Rogers City on Michigan Highway 68.

Maps: Department of Natural Resources trail map (excellent); the trail is well marked with blue blazes and signposts.

Degree of difficulty: 3-mile loop, moderate because of terrain and trail conditions, particularly along the river; the longer loops are a bit more difficult with greater changes in elevation and sandy trails in several areas.

Length: 14 total miles broken into three shorter loops of 3, 5, and 6 miles.

Elevations: Changes in elevation are often less than 100 feet, but rises and falls are often dramatic. Infrequent climbs can be strenuous.

Special attractions: Ocqueoc Falls, steelhead and salmon fishing.

Best season: Ever-present lowlands supply squadrons of mosquitos and black flies, so the trails are best avoided in late spring and early summer. July and August are ideal for family hikes. In fall, fishermen and hunters use the area to pursue their sports. Hikers should wear bright clothing—hunter orange during October and November. The trails are groomed cross-country ski trails in winter.

For more information: Rogers City Chamber of Commerce, 292 South Bradley Highway, Rogers City, MI 49779, (517) 734-2535 or 1-800-622-4148; Department of Natural Resources, P.O. Box 667, Gaylord, MI 49735, (517) 732-3541.

Finding the trailhead: The trailhead is 11 miles west of Rogers City off Michigan Highway 68. Signs will direct you the remaining 400 yards to the parking lot off Ocqueoc Falls Road. It's well marked. A map board outlines the trail loops and usually has a supply of maps attached.

The hike: The Ocqueoc Falls Bicentennial Pathway offers three loops through terrain bordering one of northeast Michigan's premier steelhead and salmon streams.

The shortest of the three loops is 3 miles and caters to the casual hiker with only moderate changes in elevation. The 5-mile and 6-mile loops share the same route, but extend farther along the Ocqueoc River through some very sandy and hilly terrain. An added difficulty is the remoteness of the outer legs of the first two loops and the entire third loop north of the Little Ocqueoc River. A good pair of boots are recommended to compensate for the variety of trail surfaces. Limestone outcroppings along the river are particularly hard on ill-prepared hikers.

36 OCQUEOC FALLS BICENTENNIAL PATHWAY

The Ocqueoc River falls, created by a series of limestone escarpments, are the largest falls in the Lower Peninsula. The mix of highland hardwoods and pines here blend with cedar bogs and swamps along the trail to create a tapestry of color, particularly in fall. Wildlife abounds along the trail, including deer, wild turkey, small game, and a variety of waterfowl. Be alert to the presence of black bear, particularly on the longer loops.

The first two loops of the system are south of the Little Ocqueoc River. Almost immediately after leaving the trailhead, hikers start to climb—a pattern that will become familiar on the outbound legs of the first loop. The climb up sandy, well-marked trails carry hikers into the hardwood highlands of the area.

The next 1.5 miles go through a mixed forest of hardwoods and conifers and lead to the junction with the shorter second loop. Hikers looking for the complete tour often combine the first two loops into a 5-mile hike by taking the connector trail to the left for the 100-yard hike toward the river and then, instead of turning left to head back to the trailhead, turning right to hike the 2-mile loop in reverse.

From the junction with the return leg of the first loop, head north for a brief look at the Ocqueoc River before reaching the footbridge over the Little Ocqueoc River that leads to the final, 3-mile loop in the system. To complete the first loop, follow the trail along the south bank of the Little Ocqueoc as it climbs back into the hardwood highlands for the return trip to the earlier junction with the second loop. You will have to retrace the short connector leg of the 3-mile loop, dropping down from the ridges to shadow the Ocqueoc River back to the trailhead.

The 1.5 miles back to the parking lot are a mix of sandy and sometimes rocky trail surfaces. The river will be a constant reminder that you are on the right track as you head back to the starting point. About 200 yards from the end of this loop you will reach the base of Ocqueoc Falls. The limestone escarpment is not a dramatic change in elevation, but a series of drops of 3 to 5 feet gather momentum along a series of deep pools. From the falls, it's an easy climb up to the parking lot. There is a picnic area at the top of the hill along with pit toilets.

Hikers who want to travel the last loop in the Bicentennial Pathway will have to return to the footbridge over the Little Ocqueoc River. Its trailhead is reached only after hiking the first loops, and is an add-on for hikers with the time and energy to complete the extra 3 miles. This section of the trail is also rated moderate, due more to the remoteness than trail difficulty. The terrain of this outer loop is similar to the first two. The outbound leg climbs onto the hardwood ridges before dropping back down to trace the course of the Ocqueoc River to its junction with the Little Ocqueoc. From the junction of the two rivers, hikers should turn east and return to the footbridge for the trek back to the trailhead at the parking lot.

One note of caution for hikers visiting the trail after September 15: the areas along both banks of the two rivers are very popular with both big and small–game hunters. Anyone hiking these trails at that time should wear bright colored clothing and avoid straying off established pathways. The segments of

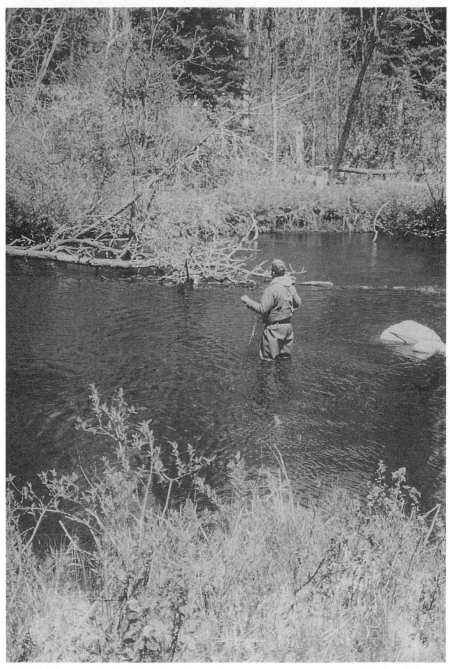

The pathway traces the course of one of northeast Michigan's premier steelhead and salmon streams.

trail that shoulder on the Ocqueoc River are high–traffic pathways during the early fall when salmon enter the stream, providing an extra distraction for hikers. In early spring, low-lying areas that trace the river may be a bit wet, requiring a detour or two, but will still be passable.

37   HOIST LAKES FOOT TRAVEL AREA

General description: 20 miles of challenging loop hikes amid lakes and solitude.
General location: Central Alcona County.
Maps: Huron National Forest Hoist Lakes Foot Travel Area map; USGS Curran and Bucks Pond quads.
Degree of difficulty: The area mixes moderate and challenging terrain that is also remote. Casual hikers should take plenty of time to navigate the loops.
Length: East loop, 13 miles; west loop, 8 miles.
Elevations: Climbs along both loops are steep. Several taller hills top out at more than 1,200 feet, but most of the climbs are less dramatic because hikers are already on ridgelines of 1,000 feet when making the trek to the highest points.
Special attractions: Wildlife, scenery, solitude.
Best season: Hikers who own snowshoes won't have a "bad" season to hike the trails of the Hoist Lakes area, but the optimum season is early fall. The weather is perfect, colors are outstanding, and photo opportunities abound. This is also the season local hunters use the area, so stay on the trails and wear bright clothing. If bugs aren't a problem for you, add this hike to your summer list.
For more information: District Ranger, USDA Forest Service, Huron National Forest, Harrisville Ranger District, Harrisville, MI 48740, (517) 724-5431.
Finding the trailheads: To reach the start point of the west loop, go north of Glennie on Michigan Highway 65 for 5 miles to Au Sable River Road, then north for about 3 miles to the West Loop trailhead.

To start on the east loop, go north from Glennie on M-65 for about 7 miles to the trailhead, or, from Harrisville, take Michigan Highway 72 west for 22 miles to the M-65 junction. Then go south on M-65 for 0.5 mile to the trailhead.

The hikes: The Hoist Lake area is managed specifically for enjoyment by hikers and other non-mechanized visitors. Mountain bikers are prohibited from using the area. The area's nearly 11,000 acres are located in the heart of Huron National Forest, offering foot travelers an opportunity to get away from the hectic pace of city life; the trails are just a short drive from urban sprawl.

The environment here in this corner of the northeast Lower Peninsula includes small lakes, wetlands, upland hardwood ridges, bluffs, and steep hills, plus extensive conifer forests. Resident wildlife includes Michigan's "black ghost," the always-there but seldom-seen black bear. The 20 miles of trails are challenging, punctuated by hills topping out at more than 1,000 feet. This is as close as many hikers will ever get to genuine wilderness. The Hoist Lake

37 HOIST LAKE FOOT TRAVEL AREA

Hoist Lake trails pass through a variety of habitats, including wetlands that stay wet throughout much of the year.

area is scenic, tranquil, and easily accessible. Trails are well marked and solid underfoot, but several hills increase the physical challenge.

The shorter **west loop** is hilly and provides access to the best fishing lakes in the area. From the parking lot, the trail heads east into the area to join with the loop about 0.5 mile away. The hike is relatively easy at first, which is somewhat deceiving because the terrain doesn't remain easy for long. At the loop junction, hikers have the option of turning south for the trek to Byron Lake, or starting the clockwise trace of the 8-mile west loop.

The clockwise hike starts out on an ill-marked trail leg that's a bit confusing but eventually becomes clear as you move away from the junction. It is a 2.25-mile trek to the next junction in the loop, the first contact with the east loop. This is a hilly, sometimes steep section of the trail, but should pose no problem for hikers who have time to proceed slowly. Hikers find themselves ridge-hopping before reaching post 11 and their first look at No Name Lake. The east and west loops share the next 2.5 miles of the system, as hikers move between marker posts 5 and 12. The trail skirts the northern and eastern shores of the lake before turning south for the final 1.25 miles of the shared trail to post 12.

There is a major climb for hikers heading toward Byron Lake, a steep ascent that puts hikers at nearly 1,200 feet and provides a great view of the area. From the ridgeline, hikers descend slightly to make the final 0.5-mile trek to the eastern shore of Byron Lake. The trail soon passes post 10 and then 9, along with markers for designated campsites near the lake. From the lake, hikers head west to the junction with the short trail spur to the trailhead and the parking lot.

Hiking the **east loop** can be done in either direction depending on how much time you have to reach a designated campsite. If time permits, hike the trail in a counterclockwise direction; if finding a campsite is highest on your agenda, head west toward Hoist Lakes campsites, about 2.5 miles away. Either way, the trail is generally easy to follow.

Hikers heading to the right from the trailhead will have a fairly easy trek for the first 5 miles as the trail traces through cutover areas and along portions of old logging roads. The path meanders through the eastern and northern sections of the Hoist Lakes Foot Travel Area, probably the easiest sections of the trail system to hike. As hikers reach junction post 5, the point at which the two loops in this system share a length of trail, the terrain begins to change a bit, becoming hilly and a struggle for those who made the long trip "around the top" from the trailhead.

Past junction post 12, hikers will make the left turn to head for the 2+-mile trek to the area's namesakes, the Hoist Lakes. At junction post 13, a spur trail leads to established campsites around North and South Hoist lakes. These campsites are less than 0.5 mile north of the main trail and are not difficult to locate.

The final legs of the east loop, a 1-mile span to junction post 14, and the final 1.5 miles to the trailhead and the parking lot, is a mix of representative habitats found throughout the Hoist Lakes area. Hills—one a climb of more than 1,000 feet—and wet marshes are strung together along this section of the pathway. More than one hiker has compared this final leg of the journey to "a final reminder of what we've gone through for the first 9 miles!"

The closer hikers are to parking lots and trailheads, the more the chance of encountering hunters during the fall months, particularly from September 15 through late November. Be aware that hunting seasons are open at this time.

38 RIFLE RIVER RECREATION AREA

General description: Quiet forest and ridgeline hikes with opportunities for fishing and camping.
General location: Ogemaw State Forest.
Maps: Department of Natural Resources area brochure; USGS Rose City and Selkirk quads.
Degree of difficulty: Ranging from easy to one notch higher than moderate.
Length: 13 miles total, on a loop running north-south through the area, with shorter loop hikes possible.
Elevations: Most of the trail system changes little, but there is one climb to an elevation just over 1,000 feet. The highest and steepest climbs are along the north loop, east of Grousehaven Lake.
Special attractions: Beauty, solitude, wildlife, birding, lake fishing.
Best season: Fall. The trail system is at its most picturesque during early

38 RIFLE RIVER RECREATION AREA

autumn as the hills come alive with color, but this is also the time of the year when hunters move into the hills and ridges to search for upland birds and white-tailed deer. Hikers should wear bright clothing and stay on the trails from mid-September until snowfall.

For more information: Rifle River Recreation Area, 2550 East Rose City Road, Lupton, MI 48635, (517) 473-2258.

Finding the trailheads: The area is 15 miles northwest of West Branch and 4.75 miles east of Rose City off County Road F-28, in the heart of Ogemaw State Forest. Trailheads for this system are located in the campgrounds on Grousehaven Lake and Jewett Lake. The Grousehaven Lake trailhead provides access to the short loop east of the lake, as well as the longer southern loop. The Jewett Lake trailhead intersects the longer southern loop between Jewett and Devoe lakes. Both trailheads/campgrounds are located off Ranch Road.

The hike: The Rifle River Recreation Area is a multi-use area that provides a quiet getaway for hikers looking for a trail system with a mix of terrain, scenery, and solitude. Once a private hunting and fishing retreat owned by the late H. M. Jewett, the area became the property of the State of Michigan in 1945. It was transferred to the Parks Division in 1963 and developed to the extent seen today.

The 4,300-acre recreation area blends nearly all the habitats and environments found in northern Michigan. Its overall beauty and solitude draw more than 100,000 visitors annually. The mix of habitat is of particular note for birders and photographers. In the northern section of the area, hikers will encounter upland hardwood ridges and the steepest climbs in the system; the southern loop is a trek through a blend of dry uplands, lake, and river habitats. The area is a haven for hunters in pursuit of both large and small game, and fishermen will find plenty of action in the ten lakes in the region.

Two main trailheads provide access to the trail system; there is also an access point in the picnic area on the north shore of Grousehaven Lake. Although you will miss the first 0.5 mile of the trail from the Grousehaven Lake Campground, it's from the picnic area that this hike description starts. Hikers will have little trouble following the first few hundred yards from the campground to this start point, but day hikers without campsites should use the picnic area.

Shortly after leaving the picnic area, hikers reach the junction with a 2-mile loop through a beautiful section of upland hardwood ridges. This hilly and often challenging loop also contains the highest point in the area, a 1,060-foot rise about one-third of the way around the loop. The ridge-hopping required for the climb to the high point becomes hill-dropping for the remainder of the loop as hikers head back to rejoin the main trail as it shadows Weir Road.

The main pathway generally follows the road and the shoreline of Grousehaven Lake as it heads south to the junction marker for a second loop trail that provides access to Scaup Lake, or the short loop's western leg, which follows the shoreline of Devoe Lake. At the end of the Scaup Lake loop, hikers head generally south along the largest loop in the area, a 6-mile trek that flanks, from a distance at times, the Rifle River.

Approximately 1 mile from the junction, a bridge provides access over Skunk Creek. This leg of the hike is not tough, but can be distracting for hikers on the lookout for photo opportunities. About 1.5 miles farther down the trail, a marker on the left points the way to Lost Lake, about 0.5 mile to the east.

Returning to the main trail, hikers take a westerly heading before reaching the first of the bridges over the Rifle River, about 1.5 miles away. You will have to cross a small creek before reaching the larger river, but it should present no problem. The next waterway is only 0.5 mile down the trail, Clear Creek. From here, for more than 2 miles, hikers head nearly due north to the second bridge over the Rifle River. This leads to rustic Ranch Campground. From the campground, hikers turn northeast for the final portions of this 6-mile loop.

Within 0.5 mile after leaving the campground, the trail crosses Ranch Road and enters a high traffic area that feeds the Devoe Lake Campground and boat launches for Devoe and Jewett lakes. This area is used heavily in summer, so be aware of vehicles along local roads. In another 0.5 mile, hikers rejoin the short loop between Scaup and Devoe lakes, this time on the leg opposite the Scaup Lake loop. A few hundred yards east on this leg, the trail reaches the northbound portion of the trail leading back to the picnic area.

Note: there is no camping allowed along the trail except in designated campgrounds. Be sure to check the park map for the locations of these sites and plan your hike accordingly.

39 PROUD LAKE RECREATION AREA

General description: Trails in lake country and rolling hills close to metropolitan areas.

General location: Huron River valley in Southwestern Oakland County.

Maps: Department of Natural Resources area map and brochures; USGS Milford quad.

Degree of difficulty: Easy.

Length: 21 miles of trails, ranging in length from a casual loop around the shores of one of the lakes in the park to the full circuit that tours all of the area's ecosystems.

Elevations: The floor of the Huron River valley is fairly flat, but there are a few rolling hills to contend with. None of the obstacles are challenging.

Special attractions: Photo opportunities, wildlife, fishing.

Best season: Year-round. Winter closes some of the trails, and others are opened for cross-country skiers only, but there is still room to roam even during this cold season. Summer is the ideal time to visit but also the most crowded. Portions of the park are open to hunters after September 15, so wear bright clothing and stay on the trails at that time.

For more information: Proud Lake Recreation Area, 3500 Wixom Road, Milford, MI 48382, (313) 685-2433.

39 PROUD LAKE RECREATION AREA

Finding the trailhead: Proud Lake Recreation Area is 3 miles southeast of Milford, and 7 miles north of Interstate Highway 96 from the Wixom exit. The recreation area is flanked by major roads, including Interstate Highways 75 and 96.

Park Headquarters for the Proud Lake Recreation Area is the main trailhead for all hikes in the area. Approaching from the south, take the Wixom exit off I-96 and drive north for 6 miles to the trailhead. From Milford, drive east on Commerce Road to Duck Lake Road, then turn right and follow the road for 2 miles to the trailhead.

The hike: The Huron River Valley in metropolitan Oakland County provides the focal point for this major recreation area just minutes from downtown Detroit. The park was established in the mid-1940s and has changed very little in the past fifty years. It continues to be one of the most utilized and most scenic of the state's recreation areas. The mix of environments provides a unique opportunity to view and photograph myriad species occupying everything from marshes, bogs, and other wetlands to meadows to upland forests that cover much of the area.

131

For hikers with fishing fever, the Huron River offers a great opportunity to catch rainbow and brown trout. The 3,614 acres of the Proud Lake Recreation Area contain blue-ribbon trout fishing. Weekend hikers will find more than enough to keep them busy: exploring nature trails, taking off on a cross-park excursion, or conveniently wandering along the river and wetting a line. Birders have the opportunity to visit nearly every type of ecosystem found in the state within the confines of the recreation area, and ponds and impoundments attract migratory birds each spring and fall.

The only real difficulty on any of the trails in the area is deciding where to go first. The pathways are easy to navigate and fairly easy to hike. The distance of the complete trail system, should you decide to hike it all in a single day, might boost the rating into the moderate category, but taken in moderation. . . . Trails and loops from the trailhead at Park Headquarters offer paths into nearly every corner of the recreation area. Short loops that shadow the rivers and lakes of the area can be linked with longer loops along the outer edges of the park to create hikes to fit your needs and timetable. Contact Park Headquarters for the latest information on each of the pathways in the Proud Lake Recreation Area.

From the parking lot adjacent to headquarters, the trails fan out across the park, many first leading through the nature study area south of the Huron River. This first set of pathways can be used as the jumping-off point for most trails in the park. Trails that trace the eastern portions of the area can also be accessed from campgrounds along Proud Lake. Horseback trails in the western end of the park are separated from hiking trails to avoid conflicts. Trails are all clearly marked and easy to follow and present no special challenge to even the casual hiker.

40   ISLAND LAKE RECREATION AREA

General description: Easy hikes near the scenic Huron River.
General location: Near Brighton and the Detroit metro area.
Maps: An area map is available at Park Headquarters. Trails are defined by blue markers, and pathways are covered by a layer of wood chips that leave little doubt as to which heading to take through the woods.
Degree of difficulty: Easy.
Length: Two loops that total 12 miles: the river loop, 5 miles, and the wider lake loop, 7 miles. A 2-mile point-to-point trail connects this park to the Kensington Metropark.
Elevations: The gentle hills will present no challenge to even the first-time hiker.
Special attractions: Huron River, urban proximity.
Best season: Midsummer. If wildflowers are your focus, late spring to early summer are prime periods. The forested areas of the park explode into a blazing landscape in the fall, and migratory waterfowl often use the lakes and river as rest stops during the same time.

40 ISLAND LAKE RECREATION AREA

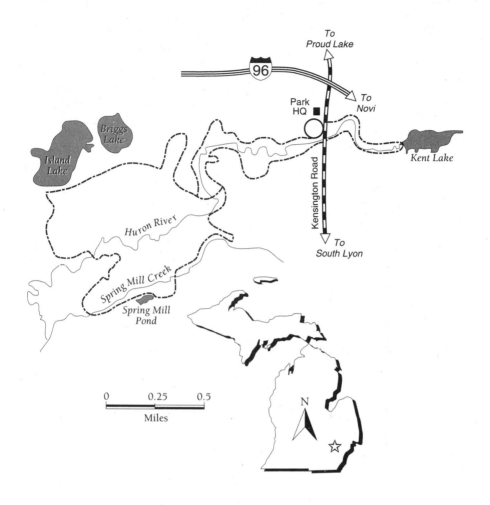

For more information: Island Lake Recreation Area, 12950 East Grand River, Brighton, MI 48116, (810) 229-7067.

Finding the trailheads: The start point for the two loops in the park is the Riverbend Picnic Area. To reach the trailhead, drive 3 miles west of Brighton on Grand River Road to the intersection with Kensington Road. Turn right on Kensington Road to the access road leading to the picnic areas and trailhead.

The hike: With its proximity to the Detroit metro area, Island Lake Recreation Area is a convenient getaway from urban sprawl. The park offers two loop trails totaling 12 miles along the flanks of the scenic Huron River. The 7 miles of river flanked by the park have been designated part of the National Scenic River program, under the Natural Rivers Act. The natural beauty of the riverline habitat makes this trail system one of the most popular in the region. The terrain provides no special challenge to casual hikers, but the beauty of the area gives plenty of reasons to stop and enjoy the scenery. Camping is available within the park boundaries for those who wish to extend their visit. The two loops in the park, although lengthy, are not at all difficult, so first-time or family hikers who have the time can easily complete either or both of them.

The **5-mile loop** that closely follows the course of the Huron River is the most scenic hike through the recreation area. It starts at the Riverbend Picnic Area, beginning in a clockwise direction and crossing the Huron River via an old cement bridge just yards from the trailhead. From the bridge it's just 0.2 mile to the junction with the inbound leg of the larger Island Lake Loop. Stay to the right on the River Loop. From the junction, the trail heads north for nearly 0.7 mile before heading to the east and the trek to Kensington Rd. For the next mile, hikers will make several slight climbs and corresponding descents as they move through the shade of mature hardwoods. About 2.5 miles from the trailhead, hikers will reach Kensington Rd. Use the road bridge over the Huron River to start the return trip along the river. For the next mile the trail shadows the Huron, bending away for 1.3 miles before returning to the bank of the river for the rest of the hike back to the trailhead at Riverbend.

The longer **Island Lake Loop** starts behind the restrooms at the picnic area. The trail's first landmark appears quickly: hikers must pass under a railroad bridge before reaching the northern bank of Spring Mill Creek. The pathway turns west along the creek and crosses the creek about 0.5 mile later. Hikers can use a bridge to reach the other side. The trail to this point is flat, but hilly terrain appears just beyond Spring Mill Pond. There are several steep hills along this stretch, so take your time as you move toward Placeway Picnic Area to the north.

After leaving the picnic area, you will cross the Huron River via a road bridge, then climb to a ridge above the river. The trail continues north until intersecting the railroad tracks, then shadows the rail line for about 0.8 mile. It bends away from the tracks for about 0.7 mile, courses through a meadow, then returns to the tracks for the final eastward run toward the trailhead. Just yards from the end of the long loop, hikers cross a cement bridge, then head in to the trailhead.

General description: A nature trail through Lake Gogebic backcountry.

General location: Gogebic County, the Upper Peninsula's most western county.

Maps: Lake Gogebic State Park brochure and map.

Degree of difficulty: Easy, with only one small hill to climb right at the start of the hike. Weather affects the condition of the trail and can make the footing in some areas rather soggy.

Length: 3 miles.

Elevations: No significant elevations.

Special attractions: Wilderness, wildlife viewing. Fishing in Lake Gogebic is tops for walleye and smallmouth bass.

Best season: Fall. Splendid fall colors heighten the quality of this nature trail, and the squadrons of flying, biting insects from earlier in the season are long gone. Some park facilities may be closed from October to mid-May.

For more information: Lake Gogebic State Park, HCI 139, Marenisco, MI 49947, (906) 842-3341.

Finding the trailheads: Lake Gogebic State Park is 10 miles north of the intersection of U.S. Highway 2 and Michigan Highway 64, or 8 miles south of the intersection of Michigan Highways 28 and 64. The park is just 17 miles north of the Michigan-Wisconsin border.

The nature trail provides a brief glimpse of the park's remote interior, and a variety of wildflowers like this Lady Slipper.

41 LAKE GOGEBIC STATE PARK

The trailhead is located in the day-use area at the north end of the camp-ground. From the park entrance, turn left into the campground and drive north to the day-use area and the trailhead in the northwest corner.

The hike: This nature trail through the backcountry of Lake Gogebic State Park provides a brief glimpse into the tangled beauty of the western Upper Peninsula. The park is located on the western shores of the region's largest inland lake, providing a full weekend of possibilities. The park is open year-round, and the trail is accessible anytime snow is off the ground, but some park facilities are closed from late October until May.

The 3-mile nature loop starts at one end of the day-use area and returns to "civilization" at the south end of the park. It is the only developed pathway in the state park and, in winter, transforms into a cross-country ski trail. The trail is easy to follow and presents no noteworthy challenges to even the casual hiker. Finding your way back through the day-use area and campground to your car might be the toughest part of the entire trek.

You can hike the trail from either end, but most hikers leave from the day-use area at the north end of the campground and return to the south end of the park. From the trailhead, hikers cross M-64, then Gillis Creek, climbing the only hill along the trail system and quickly dropping back to the level of much of the rest of the trail. The trail goes about 0.5 mile before swinging south for approximately 1 mile, then turning back toward the park.

The final mile is an eastward hike through thick forest, where hikers will encounter several areas that remain soggy for days after a heavy rain. About 0.2 mile from the end of the hike, the trail swings back north, crossing M-64 for the last time, then going over a small, unnamed creek before ending in the parking lot at the southern end of the park.

42   DAYS RIVER PATHWAY

General description: Loop hikes near the Days River.
General location: Central Upper Peninsula, in Delta County.
Maps: Department of Natural Resources Days River Pathway map; USGS Perkins quad.
Degree of difficulty: Easy to moderate, depending on the distance you travel. Short hikes along the first two loops are easy; adding the outer loops increases the difficulty to moderate.
Length: Four loops of 1.9, 3.8, 6.2, and 8.8 miles.
Elevations: No serious elevations anywhere along the trail, but several gently rolling hills could, at the end of a long day, seem tough obstacles.
Special attractions: Fall color, wildlife, birds.
Best season: Early fall, when bugs and other visitors to the area are few. The area is used heavily by deer hunters about mid-November; be aware of their presence, wear bright clothing, and stay on the trails.
For more information: District Forest Manager, Escanaba River State Forest, 6833 US 41/2, Gladstone, MI 49837, (906) 786-2351; Department of Natural Resources Forest Management Regional Office, Marquette, (906) 228-6561.
Finding the trailheads: The Days River area is about 3 miles north of Gladstone and the same distance south of Rapid River along U.S. Highway 2. To reach the parking area from the east, drive west of Rapid River on US 2 for 3 miles, then turn right on Days River Road. The entrance to the parking area is 0.5 mile west of the golf course. From the west, drive east on US 2 from Gladstone for 3 miles to the turn onto Days River Road. The trailhead is on the north side of the parking lot.

The hike: The Days River Pathway is a nearly 9-mile loop course through typical U.P. ecosystems, including wet river lowlands and heavily forested uplands. Hikes along the longest loop or any of the smaller loops in the area can be handled by casual hikers, yet are challenging enough to hold the attention of more experienced hikers. The area offers quiet serenity, accessible from

Hikers adventurous enough to make a brief cross-country trek will find good brook trout action in the river.

major highways. For a family hike, it is probably one of the best places in northern Michigan.

The area is simply a "walk through a forest," to quote a state forest official in Gladstone. The only history along these loops is natural history, provided by the changing faces of the terrain and varying ecosystems found along the trail. White-tailed deer and other animals can be found here, along with a large number of songbirds that are seen quite often along the pathway. For those adventurous enough to make a cross-country trek, the nearby Days River offers brook trout and other aquatic life. In fall, the area is ablaze in color, presenting photographers with plenty of opportunities to fill frame after frame.

The pathway's loop trails shadow the river (on northbound legs) and meander atop hardwood ridges that look down on the river (on the return trip). The trails are sandy, but easy to follow. Wandering off trail to get to the river could present some challenges, and is not recommended for novice hikers. Footbridges provide access across creeks, streams, and the one gorge along the trail.

The first loop, a **1.9-mile trail**, provides only a brief glimpse of the entire system, but greets hikers with a footbridge over a deep river gorge at the very start of the loop. Once across the bridge, the trail heads north for 0.9 mile to a junction with the second loop and a crossover trail that will return hikers to the trailhead. This leg of the trail meanders about 300 yards back from the Days River, but the waterway is visible at points along the way. At the crossover point the connector trail heads west for just under 0.2 mile to the returning southern leg of this loop. (A cross-country ski trail crosses through the connector trail about midway across; it shouldn't present any confusion,

42 DAYS RIVER PATHWAY

Days River

To
Brampton

To
US 2

Days River Road

but be aware that it is there.) The 0.8–mile trek back to the trailhead is through a forested area and, approximately 0.3 mile after it turns south, the ski trail crosses the main pathway once again. Continue south and you will be fine.

To continue along the second loop, extending the hike to a **3.8-mile** jaunt, continue north from the crossover trail junction. The loop's nearest approach to the river comes as the trail passes under a major power line, bringing hikers within yards of the Days River. From this point, the trail swings northwest and 0.3 mile farther on meets the junction with the third loop. A bridge over a small creek marks the turn to start the third loop, but by staying on the creek's southern bank you can continue around the second loop to return to the trailhead. Less than 100 yards from the first bridge, a second one, the junction with the return leg of the outer loops, will appear to the right of the pathway. Keep bearing left for the return trip. About 0.6 mile down the trail, hikers will again pass under the power line, just where the ski trail again crosses the pathway. It is now less than 0.25 mile to the junction with the first loop and the final return leg.

The **6.2-mile loop** continues outward at the first footbridge over the creek. The first portion of this loop goes very near the banks of the river. The trail swings southeast of the river immediately after crossing the bridge. The next 1.4 miles to the crossover trail (used to return to the trailhead) more or less traces the course of the river, but never really gets close enough to allow hikers to easily reach the water. The 0.25-mile connector swings west for the return trip to the parking lot. The final 0.8 miles of the third loop ends at the second footbridge mentioned earlier. Once across, hikers will trace the westerly edges of the first two loops to make their way back to the start point.

The fourth **8.8-mile loop** adds a 2.6-mile extension, and is the outer limits of the Days River Pathway. As the trail continues north, it will come very close to the river 0.6 mile from the start of the loop and continue nearby for 0.5 mile. Once the trail bends away from the river it signals the start of the return trip to the trailhead.

---

43 *HERMAN VOGLER CONSERVATION AREA*

General description: Forest and wetland loop hikes near the Lake Huron shore.
General location: Near Rogers City, in Presque Isle County.
Maps: The Presque Isle Soil Conservation District produces a good map of the trail systems, available on request by writing to: PISCD, 240 West Erie Street, Rogers City, MI 49779. Trails are well marked, with locator map boards at critical junctions.
Degree of difficulty: Moderate. No serious challenges, but there are a number of very steep hills along the northern and western edges of the conservation area.
Length: Four loops ranging from 0.75 mile to 2.5 miles, which can be linked.
Elevations: Changes in elevation are abrupt but less than 100 feet.

The river habitat below the Trout River Dam provides a living classroom for science students. Soil Conservation Service photo.

43 HERMAN VOGLER CONSERVATION AREA

Special attractions: Wildlife openings and grouse walks optimize wildlife watching opportunities.

Best seasons: Summer and fall. Springtime wildflowers splash color amid stinging insects. Summer wildlife and songbirds abound in the area. The Trout River impoundment comes alive in fall as migrating waterfowl stop on their way south. Fall hikers need to be aware that the area is open to both small- and big-game hunters.

For more information: Rogers City Chamber of Commerce, 292 South Bradley Highway, Rogers City, MI 49779, (517) 734-2535; Presque Isle Soil Conservation District, 240 West Erie Street, Rogers City, MI 49779, (517) 734-4000.

Finding the trailhead: The conservation area is just north of Rogers City, reached by driving north on U.S. Highway 23 for 0.5 miles, then turning left on Forest Avenue to the entrance and parking lot. A gravel road leads to the inner parking lot. The trailhead is located at the lot's east end.

The hike: The Herman Vogler Conservation Area is a constantly changing blend of habitats that range from highland hardwoods to marshes and a 9-acre impoundment that attracts a variety of waterfowl and wildlife. The area was purchased by the State of Michigan in 1986, through the Michigan Land Trust Fund, and was turned over to the Presque Isle County Soil Conservation District to be managed as a conservation education/recreation area.

The multi-use area is a 270-acre tract of public land, one-third of which lies within the city limits of Rogers City. The Trout River crosses the property for 3,500 feet, fed by a variety of smaller creeks—including the important brook trout nursery, Hartwick Creek. Forests of the area include ancient stands of cedars, mature hardwoods, and examples of forest management techniques that will ensure the area continues to flourish. The large parcel holds more than 7 miles of trails, used by hikers and cross-country skiers. Hunters enjoy outstanding upland bird, snowshoe hare, and deer hunting.

Hikers have a choice right from the start, since the trailhead for all the loops is the same. The northeast loop, a 0.75-mile, easy trail moves away from the parking lot along Trout River and back toward US 23. The terrain along

The flooding created by the Trout River Dam is a haven for waterfowl.
Soil Conservation Service photo.

Wooden footbridges cross the deep ravines near the shores of the flooding.
Soil Conservation Service photo.

this loop is generally flat, but the trail is a bit sandy in places, which can make travel tough. The loop traverses a mix of habitats including cedar swamp and upland hardwoods. This area has been left unmanaged in its "natural" state to illustrate the tangles nature leaves behind.

Leaving the parking lot trailhead in the opposite direction, hikers will travel only a short distance along the northern shore of the Trout River impoundment before climbing up a sandy hill to the crest of a hardwood ridge that parallels the northern edge of the impoundment. The first evidence of forest management can be seen here; the area has been both clearcut and select cut to improve stands of hardwoods and pine. At the end of the ridge, hikers drop into a wet area filled with large cedar trees and a few pockets of mature aspen, and cross Hartwick Creek via a rustic wooden footbridge. This area is popular with upland bird hunters and rabbit hunters in late fall. Several small creeks and wet areas are traversed along the trail, by means of wood bridges and walkways, and the route continues for about 0.75 mile before rising to hardwood ridges along the south edge of the area.

After crossing Trout River at the back edge of the property, hikers once again have a choice of trails. The left fork trail parallels the wetland area along the impoundment; the right fork winds through hardwood stands, wildlife openings, and grouse walks. Both forks join at a point overlooking the dam that created the impoundment, meandering for about 100 yards to a bridge crossing Trout River and leading back to the trailhead and the parking lot.

44   GRASS RIVER NATURAL AREA

General description: Six short nature trails in mixed habitat.
General location: Near Mancelona, in Antrim County.
Maps: Grass River Natural Area trail guide (outstanding).
Degree of difficulty: Easy.
Length: Cabin Trail, 0.2 mile; Sedge Meadow Trail, 0.7 mile; Tamarack Trail, 0.25 mile; Fern Trail, 0.4 mile; Woodland/Wildlife Trail, 2.25 miles; Glacial Plain Trail, 2 miles.
Elevations: Generally flat, with few elevations that would pose a problem to hikers. The Tamarack Trail is gentle enough to provide access to wheelchair-bound outdoor enthusiasts.
Special attractions: Hundreds of species of plants, 65 species of birds, 35 species of fish, and 33 species of reptiles and amphibians make this area a naturalist's dream.
Best season: A naturalist is on-site from mid-June until Labor Day, and this period is considered the best time to visit.
For more information: Grass River Natural Area, P.O. Box 231, Bellaire, MI 49615. Call (summer) (616) 533-8576; office, (616) 533-8314.
Finding the trailhead: The entrance to the natural area is west of Mancelona off County Road 618, or east of Crystal Springs Road. Drive west of Mancelona

44 GRASS RIVER NATURAL AREA

Grass River

Sedge Meadow Trail

Tamarack Trail

Fern Trail

To Alden Highway

Finch Creek

Woodland / Wildlife Trail

N

0   0.15   0.3
Miles

Scrabble Creek

on CR 618 for 8.5 miles to the entrance to the Grass River Natural Area. Turn right (north) onto a dirt road for the 0.75-mile drive to the trailhead. From Crystal Springs, drive east on CR 618 for 1.5 miles, then left (north) onto the dirt access road to the trailhead.

The hike: The Grass River Natural Area is a 1,000-acre mix of habitats: upland forests, fields, creeks, rivers, marshes, and swamps. Naturalists have identified more than 60 species of fish, reptiles, and amphibians here, as well as 400 different species of plants. The area encompasses the Grass River, which is a short connecting waterway joining Clam Lake and Lake Bellaire, both part of the Chain of Lakes in Antrim County. The natural area offers a close-up view of wetland flora and fauna, as well as other habitats.

Six short trails let hikers step into the area. The shortest, the Cabin Trail, is less than 0.2 mile long; the Woodland/Wildlife Trail, the longest, is 2.25 miles long. All six trails are easy hiking, requiring no special footwear or precautions. One of the trails is covered with cedar chips to make walking easy.

The **Cabin Trail** must be walked by all visitors, since it leads the way from the parking area to the interpretive building. Hikers will pass through a long-abandoned field and an old-growth stand of upland hardwoods before reaching the interpretive center and the start point for the other loops. The most prevalent trees in this first portion of the natural area are aspen and maple, but balsam fir, white pine, and black cherry are also present. A balsam thicket acts as a transition zone between the upland region and the wetlands.

The **Sedge Meadow Trail** starts behind the interpretive building and leads through a variety of wetland habitats, providing access to the Grass River off a short spur trail. The main trail passes through a mix of habitats, including a cedar swamp and the sedge meadow along the river that gives it its name. The trail crosses Finch Creek; near the crossing point, it's not uncommon to catch sight of feeding or cruising brook, brown, and rainbow trout. The insect life from the swampy area provides a moving smorgasbord for the fish in the clear, cold water of the creek. Wildlife along this trail include the occasional white-tailed deer, various small furbearers, ducks, and geese.

The Sedge Meadow Trail continues to the Grass River before swinging back to join the **Tamarack Trail**. The short Tamarack Trail is wide and barrier-free, great for those in wheelchairs. This brief loop into the Grass River Natural Area passes through mainly wetland areas and related flora and fauna. The trail winds its way back to the interpretive center where the next trail, the Fern Trail, begins.

The 0.4-mile **Fern Trail** does offer a way back to the parking lot, but the main attraction of this brief trail is that it parallels Finch Creek, offering a long look into the life along the waterway.

The **Woodland/Wildlife Trail**, one of the longer trail loops in the area, shadows both flanks of Finch Creek, upland hardwoods, and swampy areas as it passes through mixed terrain. The wildlife and plant varieties match the changing habitats. Included on this route is a small pond that is a viewing area for amphibian life.

The final trail loop, the **Glacial Plain Trail**, is a 2-mile hike that affords hikers the chance to walk their own way: the marked trail ends in an open field that faces terraced hills and upland forest types. After some exploration, return to the last marked sections of the trail and hike the remainder of the Glacial Plain Trail back to the parking lot.

45 PINTAIL POND NATURE TRAIL

General description: A self-guided interpretive hike in pond habitat.
General location: West of the Rifle River Recreation Area (see Hike 38).
Maps: Department of Natural Resources map and brochure, available at the entrance to the area.
Degree of difficulty: Easy.
Length: 1 mile, plus an optional loop trail.
Elevations: No significant elevations.
Special attractions: Flora and fauna along the shores of Pintail Pond and a neighboring creek. Wildflowers abound in early spring.
Best season: The area is alive in spring with wildlife, flowers, and biting bugs. If you can handle the buzzing and biting, start early. Late summer and early fall may be better times to visit. Once hunting seasons open in mid-September, wear bright clothing and stay on the trail.

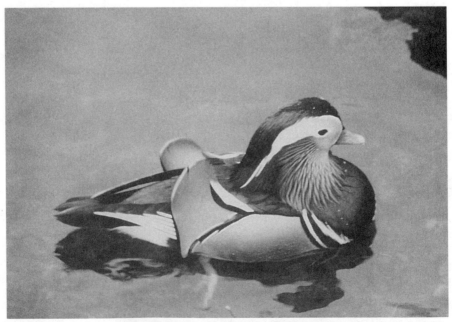

Waterfowl of all descriptions visit this area of mid-Michigan. This Mandarin duck is an exotic species, not a common site, but an occasional visitor.

For more information: Rifle River Recreation Area, 2550 East Rose City Road, Lupton, MI 48635, (517) 473-2258.

Finding the trailhead: Pintail Pond is located west of the entrance to the Rifle River Recreation Area. The area is situated 0.75 mile south of Lupton and 4.75 miles east of Rose City, off County Road F-28. From the entrance to the recreation area, turn right onto Ranch Road. The trailhead for the Pintail Pond Nature Area is across from the campground, in approximately 0.5 mile.

The hike: Pintail Pond offers a self-guided nature trail looping around watery lowlands and nearby Gamble Creek. The trail is a part of the 13-mile trail system known as the Rifle River Recreation Area (see Hike 38).

The trail is an easy hike even for the casual hiker, passing through mixed habitat approximately 1 mile north of the Rifle River. Terrain is generally flat, presenting no obstacles to hikers regardless of experience. Wear comfortable shoes.

Hikers will pass by nearly two dozen signposts, pointing to a variety of environments. Those who are equipped with the brochure provided at the entrance to Pintail Pond will head west (left), entering the first of the mixed stands of hardwoods and softwoods found in the region. The floor of these stands (predominantly white birch) is covered with bracken and flowering ferns, laced together by mats of tag alder. This is the high shoulder of the area.

Large white pines make their appearance as hikers move along the west side of the nature trail. Many of these trees were overlooked by loggers at the turn of the century, but have since grown to impressive sizes. Next, the clear, cool waters of Gamble Creek come into view. This premier trout stream is open during fishing season, offering good opportunities for brown trout. Lowlands indicate that hikers are nearing the shores of Pintail Pond. Cedar lowlands are common here, particularly white cedar.

Rising out of the lowlands area, the trail soon is flanked by stands of aspen. It is not uncommon at all to see deer and upland birds in this area because the aspen are prime browse for big game and provide cover and food for grouse and woodcock. Hikers should stay on the established trail, since areas of vegetation are simply floating above hidden pockets of water. As the pond becomes more choked by vegetation, these areas are more prevalent and pose a danger to hikers who wander off trail. Step carefully.

The lowland bog offers a compressed look at a wide variety of plants and flowers, including mosses, sundew, yellow pond lilies, and pitcher plants. This is a great opportunity to photograph plants and birds attracted to the mix of habitats.

The short hike back to the start point is through a stand of tamarack and black spruce, matching the climb out of the wetland area. Remember to take only pictures and keep footprints on the trail to avoid damaging the fragile nature of the area's wetlands.

General description: A brief walk into the history of the Civilian Conservation Corps at the old state nursery.

General location: West of Roscommon, on the north shore of Higgins Lake.

Maps: A brochure and separate map are provided by park officials.

Degree of difficulty: Easy.

Length: 1.5-mile loop.

Elevations: Level.

Special attractions: Human and natural history.

Best season: Snow-free months. Cross-country skiers take over the area in winter, but the rest of the year is left to hikers. Early spring means bugs.

For more information: Park Supervisor, North Higgins State Park, 11511 West Higgins Lake Drive, Roscommon, MI 48653, (517) 821-6125; Roscommon Chamber of Commerce, Roscommon, MI 48653.

Finding the trailhead: The park is about 10 miles west of Roscommon, on the north shore of Higgins Lake. From the north, the loop is about 10 ten miles south of Grayling off Old U.S. Highway 27. The trailhead is adjacent to Park Headquarters. From Roscommon, take County Road 203 west for 10 miles to the headquarters building. From US 27, take the Roscommon exit east for 1 mile to the headquarters entrance.

Wildflowers, such as the wild honey suckle, are springtime's treat for hikers along the course of this brief nature trail.

46 OLD NURSERY TRAIL

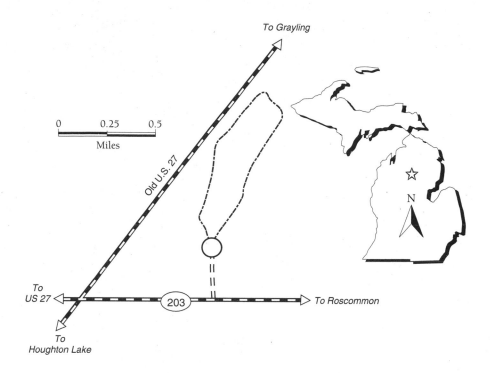

The hike: The self-guided Old Nursery Nature Trail is a 1.5-mile loop through the remains of a seven hundred-bed tree nursery area supplied state and private planting efforts in the early 1900s.

The largest appeal of this quiet area is the forest, but the rich history preserved here receives the most attention. On the south side of CR 203, just east of the trailhead, is the Ralph MacMullan Center, built by Civilian Conservation Corps (CCC) troops in the 1920s. This CCC museum site contains historic buildings, a fire tower, and other displays.

The Old Nursery Trail is a brief visit through various stations in the old state nursery. The twenty-three signposts along this self-guided trail make this an enjoyable 1.5-mile loop. The trail can be hiked clockwise or counterclockwise; the trail description given here follows the signposts to avoid confusion. Starting at the trailhead: Signpost 1 indicates the newly constructed and recreated Civilian Conservation Corps Museum.

Signposts 2 and 3 detail the area once covered by the seven hundred-bed seed nursery used to start seedlings exported from the facility, and more of the nursery grounds.

Signpost 4 notes the remains of the irrigation and sprinkler system used to water the seedlings and seedbeds.

Signpost 5 marks the site of the nursery's ice house, circa 1912. Signpost 6 shows the packing house where seedlings were bundled for shipment.

Signpost 7 indicates a 1913 model fire tower.

Signposts then move into the forest. Signpost 8 is in a mature forest area, which was the actual boundary of the nursery. Signpost 9 comes with plots of red pine. The trees here were originally scheduled to be transplanted, but were not actually transplanted. Signpost 10 shows a thinned stand used to exemplify this style of pre-production grooming. Signpost 11 marks a comparison stand, not thinned at all, to show the effects of no management in a red pine stand.

The signs also indicate natural features. Signpost 12 highlights sweet ferns, common along the trail. Signpost 13 shows an area that was burned over at the turn of the century. Signpost 14 offers a view from the top of the rim above Higgins Lake, some 126 feet above the lake's surface.

Signpost 15 comes in a new growth area that has sprouted as the result of a commercial clearcut.

Signpost 16 indicates mapleleaf viburnum.

Signpost 17 shows hikers an example of a "nurse log." The remains of a decaying log feed forest growth. Signpost 18 gives another example of the natural selection process in the forest.

The steel fire tower that once stood at the site of Signpost 19 is the same one that has been reconstructed in the CCC Museum area near the trailhead.

Near this site of Signpost 20 are the remains of the 105,000-gallon concrete cistern that supplied water for the irrigation system for the nursery.

Signpost 21 is a "take a break" point that encourages visitors to listen for the sounds of the forest.

Signpost 22 describes jack pine, one of this area's most common species. Signpost 23 points to the black locust, an important food source for small animals.

After you've passed all the above signs, you've made the loop. Your next stop is the CCC Museum and the trailhead.

47   TOBICO MARSH TRAIL

General description: A 4-mile loop near a lagoon in a state game area.
General location: North of Bay City, near Bay City State Park.
Maps: Tobico Marsh State Game Area map, provided at the nature center; USGS Kawkawlin quad.
Degree of difficulty: Easy.
Length: 4 miles.
Elevations: No noticeable changes in elevations, other than climbs up two observation towers along the eastern edge of the lagoon.
Special attractions: Wildlife viewing.

47 TOBICO MARSH TRAIL

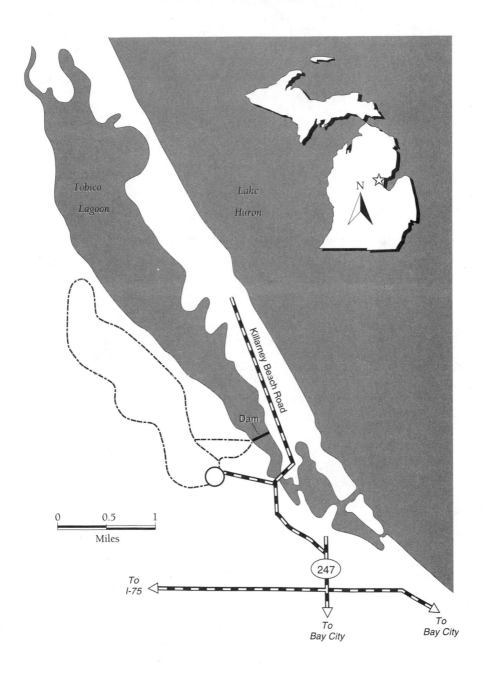

Best season: Fall months draw larger numbers of visitors to view and photograph thousands of migrant waterfowl, shorebirds, and songbirds.

For more information: Department of Natural Resources, Bay City State Park, Park Supervisor, 3582 State Park Drive, Bay City, MI 48706, (517) 684-3020. Or call the district wildlife biologist in Clare at (517) 386-7991.

Finding the trailhead: The Tobico Marsh State Game Area is 5 miles east of Interstate Highway 75, and 5 miles north of Bay City. The entrance to the marsh is 0.5 mile north of Bay City State Park.

From I-75 take Exit 168 and go east on Beaver Road. The entrance to Bay City State Park and the Nature Center is 5 miles from the exit on Killarney Road, just past the junction of Beaver Road and Michigan Highway 247. The trailhead for the Tobico Marsh State Game Area is 0.5 mile north of the Nature Center.

The hike: The Tobico Marsh wetland habitats are home to varied wildlife, and more than two hundred species of birds. DNR biologists estimate that as many as six thousand ducks and geese filter through the marsh as they migrate south in the fall. The area also offers a glimpse of rare Michigan flora and fauna that's only duplicated in larger, remote marshes in northern Michigan. Deer, beaver, mink, muskrat, more than a dozen species of ducks and geese, more than one hundred species of songbirds and shorebirds, plus rare wildflowers and shrubs can all be found in the area.

Located nearly within Bay City, the area is adjacent to some of the finest offshore waterfowl hunting opportunities in the state of Michigan. Once the private possession of a hunting club that never boasted more than ten members, the area now belongs to the people of the state.

The centerpiece of the area, the 900-acre Tobico Lagoon, provides the backdrop for this nature hike, and is the magnet that draws animals and birds to the area. The 4-mile walking loop along the lagoon's western shore lets hikers peer into the life of the marsh. It's an easy hike for all members of the family, regardless of experience. Good footwear is recommended.

From the trailhead, hikers will go less than 0.5 mile to a short loop trail and detour that leads to a dike; this side jaunt affords hikers a great view of one of the lagoon's cattail marshes at the southern end of Tobico Lagoon, and is an excellent viewing and photo site for numerous species of birds. The hike out to the dike is not a loop, so you will need to retrace your steps to return to the main pathway. Before reaching the main trail, you will pass the first of the observation towers in the marsh.

There is nothing complicated about the hike on the main trail—it's simply a scenic walk around Tobico Marsh. Nearly 1 mile from the junction with the short spur to the dike, hikers will reach the Tobico Marsh Interpretive Area. The area is a great spot for a break; it features a second observation tower and a boardwalk offering a look into the center of the lagoon.

From the "break area," it's nearly 1.5 miles around the back side of the refuge. Hikers will have plenty of opportunity to view birdlife. According to state waterfowl biologists, the marsh is a major stopover for ducks and geese migrating along the Lake Huron shoreline. Hikers enter a wooded area just about 1 mile before they complete the loop and reach the trailhead. For many hikers, this is just enough time to decide whether to make a second circuit, another trip to the dike, or plan a return visit when waterfowl viewing is at its peak.

48   SLEEPER STATE PARK

General description: Short trails in Michigan's "Thumb" region near Lake Huron.
General location: Huron County.
Maps: Department of Natural Resources Albert E. Sleeper State Park map and self-guided trail brochures; USGS Rush Lake quad.
Degree of difficulty: Easy, but footing can be tough in some areas because of sand.
Length: Deer Run Trail, 2 miles; Ridges Nature Trail, 1.5 miles; Mile Circle Trail, 1 mile; Outdoor Center–Beach Trail, 0.3 mile.
Elevations: The trails meander through rolling terrain, with no difficult or challenging climbs or descents.
Special attractions: Lakeshore scenery, birding opportunities.
Best season: Early fall. Summer may seem like the obvious choice because of the warmer temperatures, but crowds, especially on weekends, can make

A variety of species of wildlife, such as the opossum, abound in the mix of ecosystems in the park.

the season a hectic one. After Labor Day, the park population thins out and the campground and trails become a private oasis for hikers. Be sure to add a hike down the beach to your plans because the region is a major flyway for all sorts of ducks, geese, and shorebirds. The area is open to hunters after September 15, so wear bright clothing and stay on the trails.

For more information: Albert E. Sleeper State Park, Caseville, MI 48725, (517) 856-4411.

Finding the trailheads: The park is reached from the west by driving 5 miles east of Caseville on Michigan Highway 25 to the entrance. The day-use area is on the left, and the campground and trail system are on the right. Visitors arriving from the east can reach the park by driving 12 miles west from Port Austin on M-25.

Each of the four trails is accessible from both the campground and Outdoor Center, but the campground trailhead is the easiest to access. From M-25, turn south into the campground. The trailhead is located between sites 66 and 68. Parking in the campground is limited to those occupying campsites, so park in the day-use area if you plan to visit for just the day.

The hikes: This heavily forested state park offers the best of all situations for a vacationing hiker, with more than 1,000 acres of forest to explore and the beauty and expanse of the Lake Huron shoreline just a short walk out of the trees. The park is divided by M-25, with the day-use area and beaches to the north and the campground and nature trails to the south of the highway. The area's 280 campsites attract plenty of use during the summer, but the heavy pine forest separates the activity in the campground from the serenity of the woods. Set back in the park is an outdoor center off State Park Road, offering an opportunity for large groups of nature lovers to avoid crowded areas nearer the highway.

The park's hiking trails go through mature forest, over sand dunes, and through open areas with a mix of grasses and shrubs. The trails are generally empty, and offer a great opportunity to view and photograph a mix of ecosystems and species, since the terrain attracts a great many birds and wild creatures, including white-tailed deer. The 4 miles of prepared and marked trails are the only designated pathways, but adventurous hikers are free to explore where they choose in the park.

The area's one linear trail, the **Outdoor Center-Beach Trail**, is a 0.3-mile pathway that, as its name implies, connects the Outdoor Center with the rest of the park and, more importantly to some, the half-mile of beach on the north side of M-25. This trail also provides access to the 2-mile loop known as **Deer Run Trail**, which makes the deepest intrusion into the interior of the park.

From the campground south of M-25, the trail between campsites 66 and 68 provide access to the **Mile Circle Trail**, offering a brief look into the nature of the park without requiring a major commitment. The final trail, the 1.5-mile **Ridges Nature Trail**, is a brochure-equipped, self-guided nature trail reached by hiking south along the Mile Circle Trail for 300 yards. The loop passes through the diverse ecosystems that make up Sleeper State Park. After completing the nature trail, hikers can either backtrack along the Mile Circle Trail, continue the transit, or detour south at the junction with the linear trail and take in the Deer Run Trail. The point of decision is a junction less than 200 feet from the end of the nature trail.

General description: A walk in the northwoods within easy driving distance of major metropolitan areas in eastern Lower Michigan.
General location: Near Bridgeport and Saginaw.
Maps: Price Nature Center trail map brochures.
Degree of difficulty: Easy.
Length: Deer Run Trail, 0.7 mile; White Oak Trail, 1 mile; Cottonwood Grove Trail, 1 mile.
Elevations: No significant rises.
Special attractions: Beech and maple forests, birding opportunities.
Best seasons: Spring, summer, and fall. During winter, the trails are transformed into cross-country ski trails.
For more information: Price Nature Center, County of Saginaw Parks and Recreation Commission, 111 South Michigan Avenue, Saginaw, MI 48602.
Finding the trailhead: The trailhead is 6 miles south of Saginaw on Sheridan Road.

The hike: The three trail loops in the Price Nature Center will appeal to many hikers. The mix of habitat attracts birds and wildlife, and the gentle nature of the trails makes this area an easy one-day outing. The forest contains beeches and maples that are 200 years old. All three trails share the same start point, but traverse different habitats.

The first, the **White Oak Trail**, is a 1-mile loop with a connector trail that can be used to cut about 0.2 mile off the hike if you decide to head back early. From the trailhead, the hike begins to the right. Hikers will find the going easy as they enter the newest part of the forest, filled mostly with birch and aspen. After a few hundred yards, the forest changes and hikers enter a mature stand of maple and beech that has been untouched for nearly 200 years. A signpost on the left will mark the turn for the connector trail, but the main trail continues to a trail shelter located at about the halfway point in the loop.

The connector trail re-enters the loop about 0.25 mile from the shelter as you pass through more forest. The start of the Cottonwood Grove Trail loop is less than 100 yards from this junction. The junction gives you two options: head back the remaining 0.25 mile to the trailhead, or make the right turn, cross a small footbridge over a small creek, and start on the **Cottonwood Grove Trail**.

This trail loop shadows the creek for several hundred yards before turning into the forest. Its first junction with the Deer Run Trail offers hikers the option of extending the hike to include this 0.7-mile loop. Cottonwood Grove continues on around, passing the other end of the Deer Run Trail and stopping at a trail shelter that marks the halfway point of this loop. From here the trail moves onto a boardwalk because of the mucky nature of the soil along this stretch. The boardwalk extends for nearly 0.25 mile before the trail turns back toward the creek on a trail that is dry and a bit sandy.

The **Deer Run Trail** offers perhaps the best opportunity to observe the

49 PRICE NATURE CENTER

Deer Run Trail

Creek

Cottonwood Grove Trail

White Oak Trail

0   0.25   0.5

Miles

N ☆

To Saginaw

To Reese

Sheridan Road

wildlife of the area. Just over 100 yards from the junction with Cottonwood Grove Trail, this loop stops at an observation platform that is popular with birders and other wildlife watchers. The trail then follows a section of railroad tracks for more than 0.3 mile. This stretch of the loop is a favorite feeding area for a variety of birds because of the berry bushes and other flowering shrubs found along the trail. From here, the trail turns back left for 0.3 miles and rejoins the Cottonwood Grove Trail.

Total hiking time for all three loops is a casual two and a half hours, allowing plenty of time to observe the beauty of the Price Nature Center. Note: there is camping on the north end of the complex, but it is for organized groups only, available by reservation.

General description: Various loops and spur trails in a nature preserve rich with birdlife.

General location: Near Flint, in Genesee County.

Maps: The Genesee County Parks and Recreation Commission supplies all visitors with an outstanding map.

Degree of difficulty: Easy.

Length: 6.7 miles of trails in the preserve and arboretum, with plenty of chances to create hikes of any length.

Elevations: No noticeable changes in elevations.

Special attractions: Birding, and the Croyden Foote Bird Collection; wildlife viewing.

Best season: Spring, summer, and fall, because of the presence of birds and wildlife, but the park is accessible for much of the year.

For more information: For-Mar Nature Preserve, G-5360 East Potter Road, Burton, MI 48509, (313) 789-8548.

Finding the trailheads: For-Mar is within 1 mile of Flint, just west of Belsay Road. The main entrance is located on East Potter Road, and there is a pedestrian entrance along the park's western boundary, off Genesee Road. To reach the main entrance, drive east from Flint on Interstate Highway 69 to Belsay Rd., then go north 2 miles to Potter Rd. and turn left, on East Potter Rd. Go

Wildflowers and berries, such as wintergreen, paint vivid splashes of color throughout the preserve.

50 FOR-MAR NATURE PRESERVE

0.3 mile to the entrance. The main trailhead is on the south side of the DeWaters Education Center, just inside the main entrance to the park.

The hike: For-Mar is Genesee County's finest example of what caring and concern can create in a highly urbanized area. The park's 380-acre wildlife preserve and arboretum were opened in 1970 by the Genesee County Parks and Recreation Commission. For-Mar contains nature study areas, trails, and an arboretum for developing trees, vines, and shrubs planted in the park.

The preserve is visited annually by thousands of hikers, birders, and urban residents just looking for open space. Only 1 mile from the city limits of Flint, For-Mar is an active education and environmental study center, open to everyone.

The Genesee and Michigan Audubon clubs have joined together to sponsor the Croyden Foote Bird Collection, a must–stop for visitors. The exhibit is located in the interpretive building on the west boundary of the preserve. There is always a great deal of birdlife in the area. The ponds and floodings attract few waterfowl, but the woodlands and wetlands draw a wide variety of songbirds to the park. Hikers have plenty of opportunities to photograph the dozens of species that regularly visit the area, particularly along the trails that shadow the creek dividing the preserve nearly in two. In season, wildflowers paint a vivid backdrop.

The nearly 7 miles of trails in the nature preserve trace the shorelines of ponds and floodings as well as the banks of Kearsley Creek, offering visitors a close-up look at water-related habitats. The trails are all easy to follow and allow for plenty of side trips to all corners of the park.

From the trailhead at the DeWaters Education Center, the first loop is the **Edge of the Woods Trail**. This short loop traces the southern edge of Run-off Pond, but stops short of actually entering the wooded area along the creek. It is primarily a walking trail, not an exploring trail.

The **Sugar Bush Trail**, along the eastern banks of Kearsley Creek, joins other loops to create a long loop along both flanks of the waterway. Bridges provide dry foot crossings of the creek as hikers add the loops created by the **Hawthorne**, **Ground Water Pond**, **Succession**, **Short Loop**, and **Young Wood** trails to extend the hike into a nearly 7-mile trek through the preserve.

From the end of the Short Loop Trail, hikers can stop and visit the Audubon Bird Exhibit near the west entrance to the preserve. A short hike south along a paved access road will bring hikers to the other must-see point in the park—the 113-acre Arboretum, in the preserve's southwest corner. Grass- and dirt-covered trails make walking easy, and trail markers make finding your way around For-Mar a simple task.

51 WOLDUMAR NATURE CENTER

General description: Trails and wildlife viewing near the center of Lansing's urban area.

General location: Eaton County, southwest of Lansing.

Maps: Woldumar Nature Center map and brochure, supplied on site.

Degree of difficulty: Moderate. Several areas, particularly the southern and northern ends of the trail system, are very hilly.

Length: 3 miles of trails, separated into six loops and connector trails.

51 WOLDUMAR NATURE CENTER

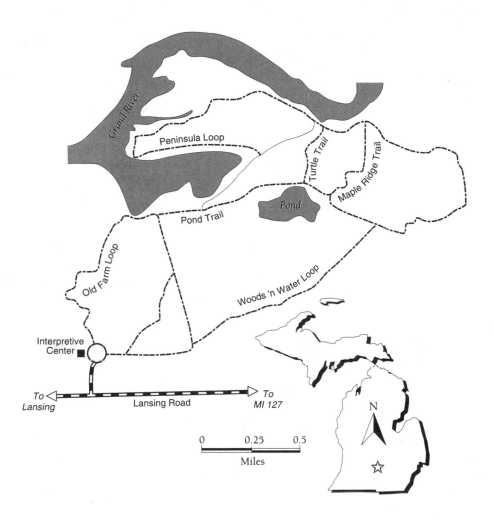

Elevations: Several steep hill climbs. Steps have been built into some hillsides to help hikers negotiate the trails.

Special attractions: Proximity to urban Lansing, wildlife.

Best seasons: Year-round, but early visits mean insects and winter means you have to share the trails with cross-country skiers.

For more information: Woldumar Nature Center, 5539 Lansing Road, Lansing, MI 48917, (517) 322-0030.

Finding the trailhead: The center is 2 miles southwest of Lansing, off Lansing Road and Waverly Road. The trails start at a point between the interpretive center and the barn south of the parking lot. Trails and loops spur off from other routes.

The hike: Woldumar Nature Center was established in 1966 when Gladys Olds Anderson donated 177 acres from her family farm to create the center. It has since expanded to its present 188 acres, and serves as a natural sanctuary for a wide variety of wildlife right in the middle of the urban sprawl of the state capitol. Woldumar contains a variety of habitats including fields and orchards, conifers, hardwoods, and ponds as well as 1 mile of frontage on the Grand River. It is an escape from the hustle of the city without making a long drive, and many who visit feel that they are "up north."

Deer, fox, raccoon, other animals, and dozens of species of birds live in the preserve. Woldumar's habitats are all left to the whims of nature, which continuously improves the complexion of the preserve. The old farmlands have begun to revert back to natural seedings; the pine plantations of the 1940s continue to provide a quiet break for many creatures. The area's ponds, swamps, and more than a mile of river frontage all provide a perfect setting for wildlife.

Woldumar's trails are well marked and easy to follow. Hikers can take self-guided nature trails, or take part in one of the many programs offered by the staff. The preserve includes three loops and three connector trails, all of which could be easily hiked in a single day. There are several steep hills, but steps assist you in getting over these obstacles. All of the trails are designed to expose hikers to the many environments of the sanctuary without disturbing the natural progression of lifecycles of its residents.

The longest loop, the **Woods Waters Loop**, is 1.5 miles long and runs north-south through the sanctuary, touching on virtually all of the different habitats. From the interpretive center, the trail heads generally south, first through a wooded area and then into an open field. The abandoned farm field is gradually being returned to a natural grassland; it's easy to see the progression that will one day develop a hardwood forest on the site.

The first junction with another trail is 0.6 mile from the trailhead. Here, the long loop meets the western end of the **Pond Trail**, a 0.3-mile connector trail that bypasses much of the southern end of the sanctuary. The main pathway jogs west a bit, then finishes the southward trace around a large marshy area near the southern boundary of the sanctuary. In spring, the birdlife in the marsh can be beautiful to watch and hear, but the high-pitched whine of insects can spoil the whole scene.

Once around the southern end of the marsh, the trail swings east for about 300 yards to the junction with the southern end of the **Maple Ridge Trail**, a 0.1-mile connector trail leading north to the Pond Trail. Past this junction, the pathway passes along the bank of the Grand River and, 100 yards farther on, reaches the southern end of the **Turtle Trail**, another 0.1-mile connector trail leading north to the Pond Trail.

Just a few yards farther east, the trail swings north away from the river. At this point, the main trail meets the junction with the **Peninsula Loop**, a 0.6-mile meander along one of the peninsulas jutting into the Grand River. You continue north through a wooded area for more than 100 yards, stepping out of the trees to reach the junction with the other end of the Peninsula Loop and, at the same time, catching a glimpse of the lagoon created by a backwater of the river. From this point you will hike in and out of the trees along the shores of the lagoon for several hundred yards. The eastern junction of the Pond Trail is passed just after you re-enter the woods.

About 100 yards farther down trail, the main pathway reaches a junction with the **Old Farm Loop**, a 0.6-mile route through the remnants of the old Anderson family farm. The main trail swings west along the edge of the abandoned farm field, and the Old Farm Loop swings back north about midway along the edge of the field. The main pathway continues west to the point where the trail first exited the trees at the start of the hike.

The return trip to the trailhead is a retracing of the first few hundred yards to the interpretive center. The steepest sections of the trails and loops found in Woldumar are along the eastern edge of the Old Farm Loop, and about midway along the Maple Ridge Trail. The three steep hills have steps built into their faces to assist with the climb. A few footbridges have been built to keep feet dry. The rest of the trail is wide and easy to walk. Take the time to study the map provided at the interpretive center before setting out for a day of exploring.

52 LOVE CREEK COUNTY PARK & NATURE CENTER

General description: Trails through mixed environments in Michigan's southwest corner.

General location: Near Berrien Springs, in Berrien County.

Maps: A trail map is provided by the interpretive center.

Degree of difficulty: Moderate, because of hilly terrain and the length of the trail loops.

Length: Trail loops can be brief or extended, and range from a 0.5-mile loop to a combination of trails along the southern edge of the park that extends for 3 miles.

Elevations: The terrain is hilly but not severe.

Special attractions: Birds, wildflowers.

Best seasons: Year-round.

For more information: Love Creek Nature Center, 9228 Huckleberry Road, Berrien Center, MI 49102, (616) 471-2617.

Finding the trailheads: The park is 2 miles east of the city of Berrien Springs, off Huckleberry Road. Take Pokagon Road southeast from Berrien Center for approximately 2 miles and turn left on Huckleberry Rd. The park entrance is about 0.5 mile north. The trailhead is near the entrance parking lot.

The hike: This 100-acre nature center offers a mix of environments, ranging from meadows and marshes to mature forests and a pond. The arrival of birds and the carpet of wildflowers in early spring are spectacular and provide hours of enjoyment. Wildlife frequents the park in summer and fall. Autumn colors

A carpet of wildflowers, such as wild forget-me-nots, provides a spectacular backdrop for hikers in the spring.

are stunning. The hiking trails are accessible during winter, allowing a look at complete lifecycles of this urban "wilderness."

The park is managed as a preservation and education area complete with an interpretive center, classrooms, and exhibits. There are several wooden bridges and an observation tower overlooking the park's marshy areas. Love Creek Nature Center offers 5 miles of interconnected trails that are broken down into more than a dozen loops, ranging from 0.5 to 3 miles. The possible combinations of loops can stretch a short hike into an all–day affair. Combinations of loops will take hikers through open meadows, marshland, and mature forests, and along the flanks of Love Creek. Bridges allow dry foot crossings of the creek, and a boardwalk keeps feet dry in the marsh in the southwest corner of the park.

All hikes originate at the Nature Center, which is just 300 yards west of the entrance to the park. The trail systems course through hilly terrain and wet areas, covered by bridges and a boardwalk. Trails are sandy but provide firm footing.

The shortest loop trail, the **Marsh Trail**, is only 0.5 mile long. The trail heads southeast for nearly 0.25 mile before swinging west to shoulder the park's only marsh. About 100 yards after the turn north, hikers have the opportunity to stop and climb the 10-foot observation tower overlooking the marsh. About 200 yards past the observation tower, hikers reach the junction with the loop made up of **Trails 3** and **4**, which circles a large meadow area. Continuing north, hikers will return to the Nature Center in about 100 yards.

52 LOVE CREEK COUNTY PARK & NATURE CENTER

To the north of the Nature Center, **Trails 7** and **8** move through a forested area before breaking into open terrain and tracing the northern and eastern shores of a small pond. The pond attracts birds, including wood ducks and mallards, but its heavily vegetated surface does not leave room for many species.

The long loops, **Trails 10, 11,** and **12**, cover about 3 miles along the southern edge of the park, from east to west. The trails cross Love Creek a number of times, but bridges make those crossings easy and dry. The trails loop through heavy woods consisting chiefly of maple and beech. The trails are all well marked and easy to follow, but keep in mind that the loops often offer no shortcuts, especially at the extreme western edge. Plan your day's outing with sufficient food and water, not to mention time.

APPENDIX A   *A HIKER'S CHECKLIST*

Hikers will take almost anything they choose into the woods, but often forget an essential item. Day hikers should always bring maps and water, and adequate clothing for the season. The list below offers a guide for hikers who intend to camp overnight or make extensive day trips in remote country. Take a final look at this checklist before you load your pack into the car.

Clothing

- ❒ Shirt
- ❒ Pants
- ❒ Underwear (extras)
- ❒ Wind shirt
- ❒ Vest
- ❒ Belt and/or suspenders
- ❒ Jacket or down parka
- ❒ Turtleneck
- ❒ Poncho or rain suit
- ❒ Gloves
- ❒ Hat
- ❒ Bandana
- ❒ Walking shorts
- ❒ Sweater
- ❒ Swimming suit
- ❒ Balaclava or headband

Shelter

- ❒ Tent
- ❒ Tent poles
- ❒ Rain/storm fly
- ❒ Tent repair kit
- ❒ Sleeping bag
- ❒ Sleeping pad

Cooking

- ❒ Matches (extras)
- ❒ Matches (waterproof)
- ❒ Waterproof match case
- ❒ Stove/Fuel bottles (filled)
- ❒ Funnel
- ❒ Foam pad for stove
- ❒ Cleaning wire for stove
- ❒ Cleaning pad for stove
- ❒ Cleaning pad for pans

- ❒ Fire starter
- ❒ Cook kit
- ❒ Pot gripper
- ❒ Spatula
- ❒ Cup
- ❒ Bowl/plate
- ❒ Utensils
- ❒ Dishrag
- ❒ Dish towel
- ❒ Plastic bottle

Food and drink

- ❒ Cereal
- ❒ Bread
- ❒ Crackers
- ❒ Cheese
- ❒ Margarine
- ❒ Powdered soups
- ❒ Salt/pepper
- ❒ Main-course meals
- ❒ Snacks
- ❒ Hot chocolate
- ❒ Tea/coffee
- ❒ Powdered milk
- ❒ Drink mixes

Photography

- ❒ Camera
- ❒ Film (extra)
- ❒ Extra lenses
- ❒ Filters
- ❒ Close-up attachments
- ❒ Tripod
- ❒ Lens brush/paper
- ❒ Light meter
- ❒ Flash equipment

Fishing

- ❏ Rods
- ❏ Reels
- ❏ Flies
- ❏ Dry-fly floater (silicone)
- ❏ Lures
- ❏ Leader
- ❏ Extra line
- ❏ Swivels
- ❏ Hooks
- ❏ Split shot/sinkers
- ❏ Floats
- ❏ Bait

Miscellaneous

- ❏ Pocket or Swiss Army knife
- ❏ Whetstone
- ❏ Compass
- ❏ Topographic map
- ❏ Other maps
- ❏ Sunglasses
- ❏ Flashlight batteries (extra)
- ❏ Bulbs
- ❏ Candle lantern
- ❏ First-aid kit
- ❏ Snakebite kit
- ❏ Survival kit
- ❏ Repair kit
- ❏ Suntan lotion
- ❏ Insect repellent
- ❏ Zinc oxide (for sunburn)
- ❏ Toilet paper
- ❏ Space blanket
- ❏ Binoculars
- ❏ Nylon cord
- ❏ Plastic bags
- ❏ Rubber bands/ties
- ❏ Whistle
- ❏ Salt tablets
- ❏ Emergency fishing gear
- ❏ Wallet/I.D. cards
- ❏ Money
- ❏ Ripstop tape
- ❏ Notebook and pencils
- ❏ Field guides

- ❏ Toothpaste and toothbrush
- ❏ Dental floss
- ❏ Mirror
- ❏ Garbage bag
- ❏ Book
- ❏ Towel
- ❏ Safety pins
- ❏ Scissors
- ❏ Trowel
- ❏ Water purification tablets
- ❏ Car key
- ❏ Signal flare
- ❏ Watch
- ❏ Extra parts for stove, pack, and tent
- ❏ Solar still kit
- ❏ Rubber tubing

APPENDIX B *SOURCES FOR MORE INFORMATION*

National Parks and Lakeshores

Isle Royale National Park
87 North Ripley Street
Houghton, MI 49931

Isle Royale *Queen* Ferry
Copper Harbor, MI 49918
(906) 482-4950.

Isle Royale Custom Charters
(906) 337-4993

Sleeping Bear Dunes National Lakeshore
P.O. Box 277
9922 Front Street
Empire, MI 49630
(616) 326-5134

National Forests

Munising Ranger District
Hiawatha National Forest
601 Cedar Street
Munising, MI 49862
(906) 387-2512

Rapid River Ranger District
Hiawatha National Forest
8181 U.S. Highway 2
Rapid River, MI 49878
(906) 474-6442

District Ranger
Huron National Forest
Harrisville Ranger District
Harrisville, MI 48740
(517) 724-5431

State Forests and Parks

Michigan Department of Natural Resources
Forest Management Division
P.O. Box 30452
Lansing, MI 48909-7952
(517) 373-1275

Michigan Department of Natural Resources
Parks and Recreation Division
P.O. Box 30028
Lansing, MI 48909
(517) 373-1275

Albert E. Sleeper State Park
Caseville, MI 48725
(517) 856-4411

Bay City State Park
3582 State Park Drive
Bay City, MI 48706
(517) 684-3020

Escanaba River State Forest
6833 U.S. Highway 41/2
Gladstone, MI 49837
(906) 786-2351

Island Lake Recreation Area
12950 East Grand River
Brighton, MI 48116
(810) 229-7067

Lake Gogebic State Park
HCI 139
Marenisco, MI 49947
(906) 842-3341

Lake Superior State Forest
P.O. Box 445
Newberry, MI 49868

North Higgins State Park
11511 West Higgins Lake Drive
Roscommon, MI 48653
(517) 821-6125

Michigan Department of Natural Resources,
Region II Headquarters
Pigion River Country State Forest
Roscommon, MI 48653
(517) 275-5151

Michigan Department of Natural Resources
Stephenson, MI 49987
(906) 753-6317

Michigan Department of Natural Resources
P.O. Box 667
Gaylord, MI 49735
(517) 732-3541

Michigan Department of Natural Resources
Forest Management Regional Office
Marquette, MI 49855
(906) 228-6561

Pinckney State Recreation Area Headquarters
8555 Silverhill
Pinckney, MI 48169

Porcupine Mountains Wilderness State Park
599 Michigan Highway 107
Ontonagon, MI 49953
(906) 885-5275

Proud Lake Recreation Area
3500 Wixom Road
Milford, MI 48382
(313) 685-2433

Rifle River Recreation Area
2550 East Rose City Road
Lupton, MI 48635
(517) 473-2258

Shingleton Forest Area
Michigan Highway 28
Shingleton, MI 49884

Sylvania Wilderness Visitor Center
P.O. Box 276
Watersmeet, MI 49969
(906) 358-4724

Waterloo State Recreation Area Headquarters
16345 McClure Road
Chelsea, MI 48169

Watersmeet Ranger Station
Watersmeet, MI 49969
(906) 358-4551

Nature Centers and Wildlife Refuges

For-Mar Nature Preserve
G-5360 East Potter Road
Burton, MI 48509
(313) 789-8548

Grass River Natural Area
P.O. Box 231
Bellaire, MI 49615
Summer (616) 533-8576
Office (616) 533-8314

Love Creek Nature Center
9228 Huckleberry Road
Berrien Center, MI 49102
(616) 471-2617

Price Nature Center
County of Saginaw Parks and Recreation Commission
111 South Michigan Avenue
Saginaw, MI 48602

Seney National Wildlife Refuge
HCR #2, Box 1
Seney, MI 49883
(906) 586-9851

Woldumar Nature Center
5539 Lansing Road
Lansing, MI 48917
(517) 322-0030

Conservation and Trail Groups

Michigan Trail Riders Association
1650 Ormond Road
White Lake, MI 48383-2344
(810) 889-3624

Pigeon River Country Association
P.O. Box 122
Gaylord, MI 49735

Presque Isle Soil Conservation District
240 West Erie Street
Rogers City, MI 49779
(517) 734-4000

Rails-to-Trails Program
c/o Phillip Wells
Michigan Department of Natural Resources
Forest Management Division
P.O. Box 30028
Lansing, Michigan 48909
(517) 335-3040

Maps

Department of Natural Resources (DNR)
Information Services Center
Box 30028
Lansing, MI 48909

ABOUT THE AUTHOR

Mike Modrzynski, an award winning outdoor writer and photographer and active member of the Outdoor Writers Association of American, has left footprints in more than half of the fifty states, but admits he spends much more time fishing than hiking. A twenty-year career in the U.S. Air Force enabled him to travel extensively and, ultimately, return to his hometown of Rogers City, located on the Lake Huron shoreline in northeast lower Michigan.

Mike has written more than a thousand feature magazine articles in national and international publications, authored two other books—*Michigan Steelheading*, and *Great Lake Steelhead Guide*—and contributed to two others. Love of the outdoors was instilled in him by his dad and nurtured over the years by the quiet corner of Michigan he grew up in.